A Short History of the
NEW
DEAL

A Short History of the

NEW

DEAL

BY

LOUIS M. HACKER

Co-author of THE UNITED STATES SINCE 1865
Author of THE FARMER IS DOOMED,
THE INCENDIARY MAHAN, etc.

GREENWOOD PRESS, PUBLISHERS
WESTPORT, CONNECTICUT

Library of Congress Cataloging in Publication Data

Hacker, Louis Morton, 1899-
  A short history of the New Deal.

  Reprint of the ed. published by F. S. Crofts,
New York.
  Bibliography: p.
  Includes index.
  1. United States--Economic policy--1933-1945.
2. United States--Politics and government--1933-
1945. I. Title. II. Title: The New Deal.
HC106.3.H22 1977   330.9'73'0917   77-4290
ISBN 0-8371-9609-4

Copyright renewed 1961, by Louis M. Hacker

Originally published in 1934 by F. S. Crofts & Co., New York

Reprinted with the permission of Louis M. Hacker

Reprinted in 1977 by Greenwood Press, Inc.

Library of Congress catalog card number 77-4290

ISBN 0-8371-9609-4

Printed in the United States of America

To

MORTIMER LAHM

FOREWORD

MR. HACKER, in reviewing the setting, design, and progress of the New Deal, has performed a difficult and highly valuable service. The presentation before us is balanced in emphasis, systematic and thorough, objective—but spiced with enough critique to arouse reflection and useful controversy. The method is historical, dealing responsibly with data, in refreshing contrast to the phrase-making impressionism and partisan exhortation so prevalent in the discussion of current affairs. Those who have read Mr. Hacker's chapters in the *United States Since 1865* will realize that he is thoroughly aware of the background of the governmental revolution of 1933–34. Eager students of the New Deal may be congratulated on finding so able an historian to elucidate it, a scholar whom John Chamberlain, writing not long since in his column in the New York *Times,* called "the most intelligent post-Beardian historian in the country."

DIXON RYAN FOX

Union College
August, 1934

ACKNOWLEDGMENT

THE author has drawn heavily, in some instances using passages verbatim, upon his earlier discussions of the New Deal, particularly his *The Farmer Is Doomed*, his articles in *Harper's Magazine* called "The New Deal Is No Revolution" and "Plowing the Farmer Under," and his articles in the *Sunday Review* of the Brooklyn *Daily Eagle*. To the publishers of these writings he makes proper acknowledgment.

CONTENTS

CHARTS AND GRAPHS

I. THE COMING OF THE NEW DEAL

The Election of 1932

THE depression was in the middle of its third year when the presidential contest of 1932 took place. There was, of course, no question of President Hoover's renomination and, in an unenthusiastic convention held at Chicago June 14–16—for already the signs were plain that victory was not to be with the Republicans— his name and that of Vice-President Curtis were again formally placed before the electorate. The Republican platform was a conservative document. It pledged the continuance of the gold standard, although it did speak of the calling of an international monetary conference to take up the problems of silver, international exchange, and the stabilization of commodity prices; it defended the tariff law of 1930; it promised to support any plan to raise agricultural prices provided it was "economically sound and workable"; and it had planks on taxation, veterans' benefits, the World Court, the St. Lawrence waterway, and the repeal of the prohibition amendment.

Despite a spirited pre-convention contest for delegates and the massing of opposition against the leading contender for the nomination, Governor Franklin D. Roosevelt of New York, the Democratic convention, meeting at Chicago, June 27–July 2, made its choice quickly. Roosevelt had emerged from the initial balloting a heavy favorite but the strenuous efforts of his erstwhile mentor and friend, Alfred E. Smith, to block his nomination had prevented a choice on the first three ballots. Before the fourth ballot had been taken, however, it was evident that the opposition had disintegrated when W. G. McAdoo and William R. Hearst, controlling the California delegation, ordered a switch from John N. Garner of Texas to Roosevelt; Garner, too, released his own delegation. Almost all the other delegates climbed on the band wagon, only the Smith cohort remaining loyal to the end, with the result that Roosevelt was named on the fourth ballot. Garner was rewarded with the vice-presidential nomination. The Democratic document was a model of conciseness but one under whose flag almost any Democrat could have sailed. It unequivocally pledged the party to repeal of prohibition and to the legalization of beer; and it promised a reform of the banking system, regulation of the stock and commodity exchanges, a federal economy program, a sound currency (without saying anything of the gold standard), an international monetary conference, a "competitive" tariff for revenue, reciprocal trading agreements, federal credit to the states for purposes of unemployment relief, the enactment of "every constitutional measure" to help farmers obtain prices above cost of production, reduction in the hours of labor, the regulation of security sales, adherence to the World Court, the independence of the Philippines, and a new veterans' program. The Socialists named Norman Thomas and the Communists William Z. Foster as their standard-bearers.

Franklin D. Roosevelt was fifty years old when he was named to make the Democratic canvass. The scion of an old New York mercantile family and a distant relative of Theodore Roosevelt, he had been brought up in an atmosphere of wealth and gentility. Trained at Harvard and the Columbia Law School he had early thrown in his lot with the Democracy and having carried a strong Republican senatorial district appeared in the New York state legislature in 1911 as a foe of Tammany Hall. He had been re-elected in 1912 and in the same year had supported Woodrow Wilson at Baltimore; partly because of this, partly because of the magic of the family name, his reward had been the assistant secretaryship of the navy and at thirty-one he was occupying what turned out to be one of the most important administrative posts in Washington. His youthful enthusiasm and his fondness for the sea made him a big navy advocate; the preparedness of the American fleet, when the United States entered the war in 1917, in considerable measure, therefore, was due to the energy he displayed in pushing the program of the navy bureaucrats. In 1920 he was Cox's running mate in the forlorn contest against Harding. A year later he was stricken with infantile paralysis and a promising political career seemed to be thus suddenly ended. But Roosevelt had great physical and mental courage and, thanks also to the loyal assistance of his mother and his wife, he was able to fight his way back to health. In one sense, his physical disability was an aid rather than a hinderance to his political advance for, confined to the invalid's chair, he could properly enter into long and elaborate correspondence on the state of the Democracy and the nation with many persons whose views normally he might have been reluctant to ascertain; and through the long years of his invalidity, although out of the public prints, Roosevelt kept his name fresh in the minds of countless party workers scattered over the length and breadth of the land. There was one public appearance at New York City in 1924 when Roosevelt placed in nomination his close friend Alfred E. Smith at the Democratic convention; there was another such at Houston four years later in the same cause. Curiously enough, Smith entertained hopes of victory in this election and despite the fact that Roosevelt's cure had not yet been completed he succeeded in prevailing on his younger friend to make the New York gubernatorial contest in the hope that Roosevelt would help carry the state for the national ticket. Smith lost the state but Roosevelt won it by a triumphant majority and during 1929–32 was governor of New York.

Roosevelt was a successful but not a great governor. He carefully cultivated the public interest and he was an adequate leader of his party in the state; he made no real or original effort to utilize public agencies in the fight on the depression and, until he could no longer ignore the findings of the Seabury investigation into the administration of the popular Mayor Jimmy Walker, he refused to challenge the rule of the corruptionists of Tammany Hall and its allies in New York City. The governor of New York, whether he wishes it or not, is inevitably regarded as a presidential possibility and Roosevelt's circumspection, with respect to his political and economic positions, was in all probability occasioned by thoughts of 1932. He entered the pre-nomination contest generally regarded as an affable and charming gentleman, who spoke well publicly and was a master of the arts of conciliation; but many doubted his possession of the boldness, originality, and resourcefulness needed for leadership in a national crisis. It is true that before the nominating convention met he had made a reference to the "forgotten man," that is to say, the small tradesman, home-owner, and workingman, as the chief victim of the depression; but this was regarded as of no more significance than such public statements usually are. Roosevelt appeared a safe and sound candidate, the only real cause for concern being his physical disability.

Roosevelt's campaign, however, electrified the country. Beginning in the spring and inaugurating a speaking tour which eclipsed even Bryan's heroic feats in 1896, Roosevelt traveled more than 27,000 miles and visited almost every state in the Union; every important economic question received his earnest attention and, thanks to the assistance of a group of enthusiastic and well-informed advisers (who came to be dubbed the "Brain Trust"), he discussed with a good deal of skill the problems of the depression and the ways out. One obvious distinction between the positions of the two candidates began to emerge as the debate before the electorate progressed: Mr. Hoover attributed the depression to international causes, Mr. Roosevelt boldly conceded that many of the country's difficulties were domestic in origin. As one of his most ardent admirers, Ernest K. Lindley, subsequently phrased it: "The program of the New Deal, as originally conceived, as developed in Mr. Roosevelt's speeches . . . was essentially national. It was predicated on the feasibility of independent economic recovery by the United States, and its long-range objective was the reshaping of the American economic system." Thus, while the Democratic candidate spoke of specific questions, he did not hesitate to interlard his remarks with general promises of a reordering of our economic society. A close reading of his addresses showed that he was not hostile to the capitalist system and, therefore, in the final analysis, that he was no radical; but the operations of the system were to be hedged around so closely in the interests of the security of the workingman, farmer, and small investor and its activities were to be directed so completely to the attainment of social rather than individual ends that to many, who had been brought up on the automatic operations of the laissez-faire economy, a veritable revolution threatened. Roosevelt was a member of the capitalist class, of course, but his income had been derived largely from interest rather than from profits; it was not unnatural that the excesses of industrial competitive enterprise and the chances and penalties of the free market should appear repugnant to one who, as a rentier, had never exploited labor or wasted natural resources. To some Americans, therefore, phrases like the following promised the ushering in of a new day; to others, it was the dusk of the gods.

Every man has a right to life; and this means that he has also a right to make a comfortable living. He may by sloth or crime decline to exercise that right; but it may not be denied him. We have no actual famine or dearth; our industrial and agricultural mechanism can produce enough and to spare. Our government, formal and informal, political and economic, owes to every one an avenue to possess himself of a portion of that plenty sufficient for his needs through his own work.

President Hoover, on his part, sought to defend his administration policy as being in entire harmony with the development and genius of the American people.[1] It was then and still is commonly assumed that the Hoover program had been merely one of drift; and that in line with the characteristic position of classical economics the President had accepted drastic deflation as the only way out of capitalism's crisis. But this was not altogether true and it must be conceded that Hoover tried to be guided by a set of positive principles. His reasoning ran somewhat as follows. Capitalism was essentially in a healthy condition; the whole trouble had been caused by the collapse of a speculative stock market; it was fear that was the greatest foe of a returning recovery. The President therefore could point to the fact that he had moved to check this panic and had called together the nation's outstanding leaders of business enterprise to assist him. In the words of Mr. Soule his plan had been: "Employers were to keep on expanding their plants, ordering their materials, producing and selling. They were not to reduce prices or wages. Labor was not to rock the boat. Government, for its part, was to push public works. If everybody was assured that everybody else would act in this way, fear would be banished, confidence would prevail, and business would not lose its fundamental soundness."

The President was able to maintain, with a certain show of reason, that his party had passed the Smoot-Hawley Tariff Act, which had been designed to protect the American market from being flooded by European goods produced by depreciated currencies and sweated labor; that he had reduced income taxes, thus permitting the well-to-do to invest their surpluses in new enterprises which therefore afforded opportunities of employment; that he had sponsored the creation of the Federal Farm Board to cope with the temporary agricultural surpluses; that he had inaugurated a public works program; that he had approved the establishment

---

[1] I am greatly indebted to George Soule's excellent *The Coming American Revolution* for most of the facts in this analysis of the Hoover fight on the depression.

of the Reconstruction Finance Corporation, on February 2, 1932, with a fund of $500,000,000 and the right to borrow more money, for the purpose of making available government credits to release the frozen assets of the financial institutions and to come to the assistance of the railroads; and that he had induced the Federal Reserve Banks to adopt an easy credit policy through the purchase of government bonds, thus increasing their liquid assets. But further than this Hoover would not go and as the depression dragged on he apparently became convinced with the classical economists that deflation must run its course. He therefore was unheeding to the clamor and angry demands of distressed farmers, oppressed workers, and bankrupt municipalities; and he would not unbalance the budget or create large-scale work projects for the unemployed. There may have been logic in the Hoover program; its enemies could simply point to the fact, however, that it had completely failed.

Early indications promised a Democratic victory but the results exceeded all expectations; Hoover went down to disastrous defeat. The popular vote was 22,821,857 for Roosevelt, 15,761,841 for Hoover, 884,781 for Thomas, and 102,991 for Foster. The electoral vote was 472 to 59, Hoover carrying only the six states of Maine, New Hampshire, Vermont, Connecticut, Pennsylvania, and Delaware. The Democrats also elected heavy majorities to both houses of Congress, the make-up of the Seventy-third Congress being as follows: in the Senate, 59 Democrats, 36 Republicans, 1 Farmer-Labor; in the House, 313 Democrats, 117 Republicans, 5 Farmer-Labor. The way was now clear for the inauguration of that New Deal, the general phrase with which the Roosevelt policies had come to be associated, which Roosevelt and his advisers had so hopefully outlined.

THE FIRST STEPS OF RECOVERY

As the country waited, it seemed almost as though all the wheels of industrial and financial activity were visibly coming to a dead halt. Not only were the depths of the depression reached in the first days of March, 1933, but imminent catastrophe seemed about to overwhelm the whole economic structure. The studies of F. C. Mills and Simon Kuznets, made for the National Bureau of Economic Research, showed that between 1929 and 1932: the total physical output of goods in the country had been reduced 37 per cent; total labor income in all industries had declined 40 per cent (although in a group of industries for which data were available wages alone had dropped 60 per cent), while total property income had declined only 31 per cent (dividends had dropped 57 per cent but interest had dropped only 3 per cent). There was no bottom for the dizzying fall of prices; by March, 1933, the unemployed were variously estimated at from 13,600,-000 to 17,000,000; local public agencies (private charity had long given up the unequal struggle) were finding it impossible to carry the growing load of relief; the seasonally adjusted index of industrial production (in terms of 1923–25 as 100) in March stood at 59, that of construction at 14, that of factory employment at 59, that of factory payrolls at 37 (unadjusted), and that of freight car loadings at 50; the farmer's dollar, in terms of purchasing power, was worth just about 50 cents. The burden of public and private debts, in the face of declining prices, was becoming well-nigh intolerable and threatened to consume almost the whole income of the country; the wellsprings of credit appeared to have dried up. There was no universal clamor for direct governmental assistance, no rioting, no industrial violence; but the silence, too, was an ominous one. This was the economic and mental climate in which the Hoover Administration was slowly ticking its last hours away.

At first gradually, soon with increasing intensity, the banking system of the country began to sag and then to collapse. The initial signs of disaster were visible in Detroit when the leading banks closed; this was followed by the establishment on February 14 of a state-wide banking moratorium for eight days. But the banks never reopened and by March 2 there were twenty-one states and the District of Columbia which had come to join Michigan either in suspending or in closely restricting banking operations; the Federal Reserve system reported widespread hoarding. On the eve of Roosevelt's inauguration the panic had reached the great financial nerve centers of the nation, New York and Chicago, with the result that the governors of New York and Illinois had announced banking holidays. The day of the new president's inception into office saw banking operations practically at a stand-still in every state and with all security and commodity exchanges closed.

Roosevelt moved with celerity. His cabinet announcements contained no real surprises and occasioned no alarm. The Secretary-ship of State went to Cordell Hull, United States Senator from Tennessee; William H. Woodin, a personal appointee, was named Secretary of the Treasury (he was soon succeeded by Henry Morgenthau, Jr.); James A. Farley, chairman of the Democratic National Committee, received the customary reward of the Post Office; Miss Frances Perkins was given the Labor Department; Henry A. Wallace was named Secretary of Agriculture; the Departments of Justice, War, Navy, Interior, and Commerce went to Homer S. Cummings, George H. Dern, Claude A. Swanson, Harold L. Ickes, and Daniel C. Roper respectively. Some of the President's most trusted advisers, whom he frequently consulted individually but apparently never collectively as a "kitchen" cabinet or even as a "Brain Trust," included Raymond Moley, Assistant Secretary of State; Rexford G. Tugwell, Assistant Secretary of Agriculture; Henry Morgenthau, Jr., head of the Federal Farm Board; William Phillips, Undersecretary of State; and Lewis W. Douglas, Budget Director. Professor Felix Frankfurter of Harvard, considered by many as the inspirer of a considerable part of the President's New Deal program, did not figure officially in the Administration. Bernard M. Baruch, also as a private citizen, was believed to be very close to the President.

On March 5 President Roosevelt ordered every bank in the nation closed for four days and placed an embargo on the withdrawal or transfer for domestic or export use of gold or silver; on March 9, when the Seventy-third Congress met in special session, Roosevelt had ready for its consideration the Emergency Banking bill, which both houses passed the very same day. The intention of the measure was simple: it was designed to permit the sound banks to reopen and to furnish them with currency for the purpose of liquefying their assets. Its more important sections provided: that additional Federal Reserve Bank notes were to be issued to member banks up to 100 per cent of the value of their government bonds and up to 90 per cent of other rediscounted assets, that is to say, notes, drafts, bills of exchange, and bankers' acceptances; that the open market operations of the Federal Reserve Banks were to be enlarged by permitting them to lend to any persons or corporation on notes secured by government bonds; that national and state banks which were members of the Federal Reserve system could reopen only under license from the Treasury (banks not entirely insolvent were to be placed under the control of "conservators" and could operate only under restrictions); that the Secretary of the Treasury could call in all gold and gold certificates in the country; and that the Reconstruction Finance Corporation was to be authorized to subscribe to the preferred stock, capital notes, and debentures of banks and trust companies.

It is generally conceded that while the President's measure halted the progress of panic—hoarding was checked, gold flowed back into the Federal Reserve Banks, and the majority of the banks of the country quickly resumed their normal activities—a golden opportunity was missed if not to nationalize the credit institutions of the country (as many liberals hoped) then at least to force all banks to join a much modified Federal Reserve system operating in the public interest. The country's leaders were so sunk in despair that any daring act by the President would have been accepted as the only expedient possible under the circumstances. But Roosevelt's refusal to strike out in unexplored regions (it was said for him in justification that no plan permitting a bold course of conduct was available at the time) introduced the first note of doubt as to the thoroughgoing nature of the reform program he was going to inaugurate.

The second emergency measure of the Administration was the so-called Economy bill whose passage Roosevelt demanded on March 10. Pointing out that there was a danger that the 1931–32 deficit of $2,885,400,000 might grow to almost twice that size by the end of the fiscal year 1933–34, the President insisted that a first step to national recovery was the balancing of the budget. This was to be effected in two ways: by drastic governmental salary cuts, and by a sharp paring down of the benefit payments under the veterans' pension system. The President asked for the right to reduce up to 15 per cent all federal salaries and to reorganize the pension system on the bases of service-connected disability and the permanent disability of veterans in civil life; this program would save the government $500,000,000. In the face of grumblings of federal employees, the lobbying of veterans' organizations, and the defection of many Democratic congressmen, the bill was passed by both houses and on March 20 received the President's signature.[2]

[2] The Economy Act made far-reaching changes in the veterans' pension system. It repealed existing laws relating to benefits for World War and Spanish War

A third recovery act, signed March 22, was the legalization of beer and wine with an alcoholic content of 3.2 per cent by weight, largely in the interests of obtaining additional revenue. A fourth, this one designed to cope quickly with more obvious aspects of the unemployment problem, was the signing on March 31 of a bill setting up the Civilian Conservation Corps. This agency was to put to work at once on reforestation, road building, and flood control projects some 250,000 unemployed citizens who were to be housed in special camps, paid $30 monthly, and were to be under the supervision of army officers. With immediate emergency questions thus out of the way the more enduring parts of the program were now ready for submission to Congress. Before these are to be examined, however, it is proper that some attention be given to the theory of reconstruction that, presumably, was at the heart of the New Deal legislation.

THE NEW DEAL NO REVOLUTION

Since the New Deal has been described as a revolution by its opponents from the right and even by some of its defenders, it is important that its real nature be subject to analysis. The natural history of revolutions in modern times has amply demonstrated that they are relatively simple affairs. An economic society in its youth is one of very great vigor; not only has its tone been set by a leading class freshly emerged from triumphant struggle, but its purposes have also had the sympathy and support of nearly

veterans and authorized the President to establish a new pension system within broad limits. Four veterans' groups were entitled to pensions: (1) veterans with service-connected disabilities; (2) veterans with non-service-connected disabilities where such disabilities were permanent; (3) widows and children of those who served in any war since the Civil War, except the World War; (4) widows and children of men who died as a result of service-connected injuries. The act retained on the pension rolls, under mandatory provisions, all veterans actually disabled in the World War, and Spanish War veterans to whom pensions had been granted because of age. The President was authorized to make regulations granting pensions, fixing degree of disability, and prescribing service connection.

In the only revolt against Roosevelt's leadership Congress, on March 28, 1934, passed over the Presidential veto the Independent Offices Appropriations Act which not only called for the restoration of the 15 per cent pay cut of federal employees but also provided more liberal benefits for veterans for the remainder of the fiscal year 1934 and the entire fiscal year of 1935. In this act Congress restored a form of veterans' benefit—that covering the so-called presumptive disability (i. e., the burden of proof that the disability was *not* service-connected rested with the government)—which Roosevelt had refused to include in the Economy Act. There were some 29,000 veterans in this category.

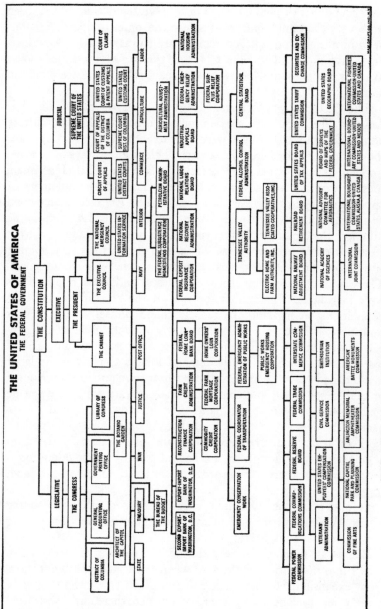

THE UNITED STATES OF AMERICA
THE FEDERAL GOVERNMENT

THE NEW DEAL AGENCIES IN THE FEDERAL GOVERNMENT

all groups in the population. The old vestigial traces have been cut away, class antagonisms—because the opportunities for enterprise in hitherto unexplored regions are so many and so bewildering—have not yet had time to form; the life of the times moves to a new harmony in which what dissonances there are are faint and unimportant.

The histories of Victorian England and of post-Civil War America are excellent cases in point: industry thrived, culture flourished, and class lines were in flux because new outlets for the energies of the ingenious and the bold were always appearing. Cobden, Bright, Rhodes, Rockefeller, Carnegie, Hill, Harriman, sons of working and lower middle-class families, found doors of opportunity open wherever they turned. The English factory hand or agricultural laborer could escape to Lancashire, London, or the colonies; the American farmer, mechanic, or small tradesman went west and made his fortune as a land speculator, merchant, mining or railroad promoter—it hardly mattered what the method was. There was an easy flow between classes, and class relationships were in balance. The farmer, because of the pressure by growing populations on his land, frequently found himself the owner of a property whose value kept constantly mounting: he could generally sell out and realize on the unearned increment. The skilled worker, because of the steady demand for his services in the labor market, had his price and it allowed him to maintain a high level of subsistence and to put something aside toward the day when he could open his own small plant. The horizons of capitalism appeared limitless (at any rate, to all but the very lowest substandard workers in the industrial economy; and even these could dream of opportunity—through the enchanted gate of public education—for their sons): there were railroads to be built, mines to be opened, forests to be leveled, street railways, water works, sewerage systems, and public utility plants to be constructed in every country of the Western world and in many of those not yet recognizing the blessings of civilization.

But as an economic society during the course of its evolution grows into maturity and old age: when the leading problem shifts from expansion into new fields to consolidation of those already won: when for the living energies of men there are substituted institutional patterns: class lines harden. Then oppression becomes the unconcealed weapon of the ruling group and class hostilities are unmasked. Revolution is a device employed by society for the destruction of the constricting molds of such class relations; it wipes them out once and for all and commutes their solidified forms into a new fluidity. The English Revolution, the French Revolution, the American Revolution, and the Russian October Revolution were such clean breaks with the past: the first two released the English and French bourgeoisies from the unbearable pressure of feudal and commerical aristocracies; the third threw off the bonds of a confining commercial system designed for the exploitation of the American colonies solely in the interests of the English merchant class; the fourth freed the Russian urban and peasant proletariats from the crushing domination of their feudal and industrial overlords.

Revolution and counter-revolution must be clearly differentiated. The American Civil War, launched by the slave masters of the South in an effort to prevent their defeat at the hands of the growing middle class of the North and West, was counter-revolutionary: its aim was the perpetuation of the slipping class power of the Southern planter through the destruction of his class rivals. Similarly, the Fascist and Nazi seizures of the Italian and German governments have been counter-revolutionary: in both countries capitalism, confronted by organized and powerful proletariats, proceeded to stamp out opposition, crush the working-class movements, and openly employ the force of the state to make secure its own position. What Fascist and Nazi apologists call the totalitarian state is the capitalist state pure and simple—and achieved through counter-revolutionary violence.

Obviously, in terms of these definitions, the New Deal has been neither revolutionary nor counter-revolutionary. Its rationale may be stated in the following group of propositions. The New Deal has recognized that the American economy has slowed down and that the forces within it are no longer in equilibrium. Opportunities for capitalist enterprise have contracted—the population has ceased expanding, there are no new great industrial fields to be opened up, oversea markets have been shut off by high tariff walls or are already being closely worked by hostile imperialist nations—and capitalism is actually confronted by a fall in the rate of profit. Control has shifted from industrial capitalism to finance capitalism (with the emphasis therefore no longer on legitimate economic expansion but on the exploitation of investors and the wrecking of properties); the spread between capacity to produce and ability to consume constantly widens; imperialism reveals its inability—without deadly international warfare—to provide all the needed outlets for surplus capital. The world market for our agricultural products has largely disappeared and a decline in farm land values has set in. Not only have new jobs for white-collar and professional workers virtually become non-existent, but there is a surplus rather than a dearth of industrial labor as well. Class lines have been clearly drawn; the danger of class hostilities is no longer remote but already in evidence. Under the conditions of a free market the owners of the means of production, because of their greater strength and organization, could continue to maintain themselves, perhaps for a long time; but their security would depend upon the steady debasement of the standards of living of the other classes in society.

This, it must be plain, would eventually lead to the creation of conditions favorable to either revolution or counter-revolution; but the philosophers of the New Deal, abhorring the thought of violence and having no conscious class interests of their own, have refused to agree that the mechanism has run down. They will wind it up again and, having done that, will suspend in balance and for all time the existing class relations in American society. The private ownership of the means of production is to continue; but capitalism is to be stopped from exploiting, on the one hand, the producers of its raw materials and, on the other, its labor supply. Agriculture, despite its over-capitalized plant and its virtual restriction to the domestic market, is to get a large enough return to allow for the meeting of fixed charges and the purchase of capital and consumers' goods. Wage earners, although in a machine economy there are too many of them in the white-collar and laboring groups, are to be assured employment and at least means of subsistence, if not incomes conducive to a decent standard of living.

This idea of establishing a balance between American class relations occurs again and again in the writings and utterances of President Roosevelt and his advisers. Thus, as late as March 5, 1934, the President stated the principle clearly:

What we seek is balance in our economic system—balance between agriculture and industry and balance between the wage earner, the employer and the consumer. We seek also balance that our internal markets to be kept rich and large, and that our trade with other nations be increased on both sides of the ledger.

The New Deal, to put it baldly, assumed that it was possible to establish a permanent truce on class antagonisms. The device it was going to use was the restoration of purchasing power through the application of an idea known to antiquity and the Middle Ages—the just price.

THE THEORY OF THE NEW DEAL

The world-wide collapse that set in with 1930 had been characterized everywhere by a slipping of prices. Now a decline in the price level in itself is no sign of disaster: the record of prices from the 1870's to the outbreak of the World War had followed fairly uniformly a downward course without imperiling the whole economic structure. The reasons were simple: the greater efficiency of production and the wider distribution of commodities made the element of price a comparatively unimportant factor in the economic processes. What caused the situation to take on real aspects of alarm in 1930 and after, however, was that the great burden of private and public debts, in the face of contraction of markets because of artificial trade barriers and deadly competition, could not be carried at the same time that prices were falling. According to the Twentieth Century Fund, the long-term debt of American public agencies totaled $33,000,000,000 while that of American corporations and individuals totaled $100,000,000,000. These debts were the real difficulty; to lighten them would have meant repudiation either through wholesale bankruptcy or unchecked inflation, and to avoid this dread alternative the New Deal chose what seemed the easier one of restoring buying power through the raising of the price levels.

That the raising of prices was at the heart of the New Deal program and its "definite and determined" policy can be indicated innumerable times from the statements of the New Deal leaders. Thus President Roosevelt, in the speech above cited, said:

The National Industrial Recovery Act was drawn with the greatest good of the greatest number in mind. Its aim was to increase the buying power of wage earners and farmers so that industry, labor, and the public might benefit through building up the market for farm and factory goods. Employer, wage earner, and consumer groups are all represented on its boards with the government; all three groups with the government must have the interests of all the people as their main responsibility.

A variety of factors had contributed to the continuance of the price decline once the crisis had set in. Industry, on its part, resorted to unregulated and cut-throat competition in an effort to keep down overhead and labor costs: it worked marginal plants, turned increasingly to mechanization, sweated labor, cheapened goods and methods of fabrication, and launched on intensive and in some cases dishonest advertising and selling campaigns.[3] Agriculture, with an economy geared to world production but more and more confined to a narrowing domestic market, adopted the only course open to it: it tried to produce more foods and fibers per unit of plant. Labor, confronted by shrinking opportunities of employment, was forced to sell its services cheaply and debase its standards; and the sweated industries once more began to flourish, child labor increased, children were taken out of schools, and women resumed homework. Finally, and this was an important characteristic of the crisis, the movement of long-term funds into capital enterprises almost ceased: for the agencies for such credits, the savings banks, insurance companies, trust funds of one kind or another, seeing their earlier investments unproductive, feared to assume further risks until some elements of stabilization had manifested themselves.

These were the difficulties the New Deal undertook to meet. Class antagonisms were to be charmed away by the use of the magic device of the just price, that is to say, a higher price level, all around.

---

[3] One of the most significant phenomena of the depression period was the increase of productivity. According to F. C. Mills, productivity increased from 100 units per man-hour in 1927 to 120 units in 1932, or 20 per cent.

II. THE NEW DEAL IN THEORY: RECONSTRUCT-ING AGRICULTURE AND INDUSTRY

RESTORING THE FARMERS' PURCHASING POWER

ON March 16, 1933, President Roosevelt sent to Congress the Administration bill for the relief of agriculture. Accompanying the measure, which was based on the unprecedented principle of the grant of subsidies (through rental or benefit payments) to farmers in return for acreage reduction, was a message which stated:

> I tell you frankly that it is a new and untrod path, but I tell you with equal frankness that an unprecedented condition calls for the trial of new means to rescue agriculture. If a fair administrative trial of it is made and it does not produce the hoped-for results, I shall be the first to acknowledge it and advise you.

This was the first of the systematic programs of the New Deal proper; and its early appearance indicated that the Administration regarded improvement in agriculture as the spearhead of the New Deal's advance.

Depression had set in in agriculture almost immediately after the termination of the World War; and for fully a decade, while factories hummed, labor had employment, and outlets for financial surpluses seemed inexhaustible, the growers of commercial crops were being confronted by a constricting world market. All the evidences of a depressed economy were present: prices kept on tumbling, land values dropped, carryovers of stocks piled up, tenancy, indebtedness, and the pressure of fixed charges increased. The farmers disappeared as purchasers of capital goods and cut down to the barest necessaries out-of-pocket expenditures for their homes and plants. A characteristic contradiction appeared: agriculture became more efficient as a productive system as its gross income declined.

To the New Dealers the theory of recovery seemed plain enough: restore the purchasing power of the agricultural population, which represented one-fourth of the nation's total, and we should be launched again on another wave of prosperity. The surpluses of cash crops—of cotton, wheat, tobacco, corn, hogs, rice, dairy products—were the heart of the difficulty: eliminate them, by destruction if necessary, and the state of agriculture would be healthy once more. It was not commonly recognized, however, to what extent overexpansion of farm plant was an essential characteristic of the whole American modern economy. The reasons for its extraordinary growth are important to an understanding of the problem of agriculture in the United States.

From the outbreak of the Civil War to the conclusion of the World War, American political leaders and industrialists did everything in their power to expand the operations of American agriculture. The young Northern capitalism, emerging from its triumphant struggle against the Southern slave economy, could not advance to maturity and power, behind its sheltering tariff walls, without foreign financial assistance: and it was here that the historic mission of commercial agriculture was fulfilled. The American production of foodstuffs and fibers, beyond domestic needs, was ceaselessly pushed so that our great surpluses could feed and clothe Europe—thereby balancing our international payments and building up, with the aid of European savings, our own capitalist economy.

The revival, beginning with the 1890's, of Malthusianism—that old dread of a failing food supply—was an additional spur; and this fear was at once reflected in the governmental policies of the Roosevelt and Taft administrations. It was during those years that the conservation movement, the expansion of irrigation projects, the back-to-the-land crusade, and an extraordinary increase in the budgetary allotments made to the Department of Agriculture took place. Besides, the continual pressure on the land by the dispossessed classes of Europe and our own industrial East made for a steady rise in land values so that, while periodic declines in farm prices made operations frequently unprofitable, the American farmer could continue to regard himself as solvent. Meanwhile politicians of the ruling Republican party, in order to hold the agrarian West in its unnatural alliance with the industrial East, fostered a generous public agricultural policy. The free settlement of the public domain, governmental subsidies to railroads, support of land grant colleges, and a protective tariff for the wool growers of the Middle West and later of the Far West were characteristics of the program. Finally, during the World War, as a result of the pressing need of, first, the Allies and, then, the United States itself for foodstuffs and fibers, further areas were opened to cultivation. Indeed, in the seven years 1913–20, probably 50,000,000 acres of new land were brought under the plow.

Such was the historical background of American agriculture's physical growth. As a result, there existed surpluses which the home market could not absorb and which could be got rid of abroad only with the greatest difficulty. The following were the more significant reasons why the agriculture of the post-World War period was in permanent decline.

The United States had become a creditor nation; instead of being compelled to export raw materials to pay interest on foreign borrowings, it had to be prepared to receive these on the account of American portfolio and direct investments abroad. The savings of American rentiers and the undistributed profits of American corporations were now invested in those newer lands—Canada, Mexico, South America, Africa, Australasia, the Far East—which could balance their international payments only by selling in the world market those foodstuffs and fibers which we ourselves kept pouring into Europe up to the World War. Ironically enough, not only did the United States have to prepare to be displaced in foreign markets but it faced the probable necessity of making room in its home market for imported agricultural goods to compete with those domestically produced. The efforts in 1934 to eliminate a proposed tax on foreign vegetable and fish oils was a case in point: at the demands of processors and manufacturers the cheaper oils from South America, the African coast, and the Far East were to be permitted to compete with native products derived from hogs, cotton, soy beans, and fish.

Again, many of our former customers had been completely lost to us or were definitely turning away. England was trying to favor the agricultural wares of its oversea dominions and such good customers for its manufactured products as Argentina; Italy and Germany, the lessons of the war ever fresh in their minds, were striving to attain national self-sufficiency; other nations of Europe favored the agricultural products of the Danubian countries, Poland, and Denmark in order to obtain trade advantages for their own finished-goods surpluses; Japan, trying to hold its bitterly won lead in the Indian cotton-goods market, was promising to purchase Indian raw cotton in return. Everywhere in the world new areas were being opened to cultivation—for agricultural wares are the cheapest and quickest goods peoples harassed by debts can produce.

The changed international position of agriculture can be quickly gathered from the following. Between 1913 and 1932, the United States increased its area devoted to major crops from 290,000,000 to 320,000,000 acres, or more than 10 per cent; in the same period, Europe, Canada, Argentina, and Australia combined had increased their acreage from 631,000,000 to 724,000,000, or more than 16 per cent. The crop output in the leading producing areas outside of the United States had grown at even a greater ratio, being in the neighborhood of 40 per cent. As Messrs. Ezekiel and Bean have pointed out in their study "The Economic Bases for the Agricultural Adjustment Act": "This increase in foreign competition and foreign self-sufficiency brought about a persistent decline in United States exports of food products from 1921 on, long before the 1929 collapse. The 1932–33 export volume finally shrank below prewar levels. In the face of this shrinkage in foreign demand, acreage of important crops in the United States has been maintained about 10 per cent above prewar acreage."

The situation in the United States itself was no more encouraging for a larger consumption of the products of agriculture. We were confronted by a stationary population and, therefore, a change in age distribution. Cessation of population growth inevitably implied contraction of land use; while the growing weight of an older population also was likely to have the same effect through bringing about profound changes in dietary habits. Indeed, the last two decades had already witnessed a marked shift in the foods we consumed, from a reliance on grains and beef to a greater use of pork, vegetables, fruits, milk, and sugar. The significance of this shift lies in this fact: grains and beef are largely the products of extensive cultivation; pork, vegetables, fruits, and milk are the products of intensive cultivation requiring less land in use and more capital expenditures. (The increase in sugar consumption has merely meant greater imports from overseas.) How those changes can affect land use we may gather from the following calculations (the work of O. E. Baker, one of America's leading agricultural economists). The average adult American consumes food the equivalent to 1,400,000 calories a year. To furnish this amount of energy, in terms of corn or potatoes, would require the use of three-quarters of an acre; in terms of wheat, 1½ acres; in terms of pork and lard, 3 acres; in terms of milk, 2⅓ acres of crops and 1½ acres of pasture; in terms of beef and veal, 11 acres of crops and 2½ acres of pasture. The greater the shifts are from grains and beef (and with continuing mechanization of industry, improved methods of heating homes, and an older population these shifts may be expected to continue) the less will be the land required to furnish the food needs of the American population.

Perhaps of even greater importance, as regards contracting land use, was the growing efficiency of American agriculture. In fact, between 1919 and 1929, on a stationary cultivated acreage, the output of American farmers increased more than 20 per cent! There were largely three reasons responsible for this revolutionary advance: progress in the application of mechanical methods and the motorization of farm equipment (with an accompanying decrease of land use necessary for the provision of feed grains for horses and mules); increasing acre yields as a result of intensive cultivation, the improvement of crop strains, and the application of fertilizer; and the greater efficiency of milk and meat animals per unit of feed consumed.

Such progress could be accelerated. Secretary of Agriculture Wallace, in his annual report for 1933, pointed out that every wheat farmer on the Great Plains, if he used the tractor and combine, could cultivate 1,000 acres and feed 2,000 people; that if new corn varieties, fertilizer, and efficient crop rotations were employed, the acreage of the nation's present corn supply could be cut from 100,000,000 to 70,000,000; that cotton picking machines, if widely used, would expand the acreage one man could handle from the present 20—40 to 100—200 (an increase in productivity of 400 per cent)! Efficiency in milk production had really only begun: for, in the five years preceding 1930, while the number of dairy cows had been only 5 per cent greater than ten years before, production of milk had increased 25 per cent—with an increase of feed consumption of only 15 per cent.

This was the complex situation which the New Deal sought to resolve by legislation. After considerable debate the so-called Agricultural Adjustment Act, the first part of the farm relief program, was passed by both houses of Congress and received

Roosevelt's signature on May 12. Stating as its intention the necessity to "reëstablish prices to farmers at a level that will give agricultural commodities a purchasing power with respect to articles that farmers buy equivalent to the purchasing power of agricultural commodities in the base period," that is to say, fixing the purchasing power of the farmer's dollar at 100 cents, the measure named such a base period for the basic cash crops of wheat, cotton, corn, hogs, rice, and dairy products as the prewar period August, 1909–July, 1914, and for tobacco as August, 1919–July, 1929. To attain this, voluntary acreage reduction was to be achieved by one or all of three methods; in return, farmers were to receive subsidies, funds for which were to be derived from the imposition of taxes on the processors of the enumerated farm products. That these taxes would be passed on to the consumers none concerned made any effort to conceal.

The income of farmers was to be raised through the following devices: (1) By cotton option contracts. The Secretary of Agriculture was to enter into contracts with cotton growers under which these were to reduce their cotton production in 1933 by at least 30 per cent below that of 1932 without using commercial fertilizer; the land thus taken out of cultivation was not to be used for the planting of other cash crops. In return, the cotton growers were to receive free options on an amount of cotton corresponding to the size of their reduction which was held by the old Federal Farm Board. If the price of cotton rose the farmers realized a profit by exercising their options. (2) By rental or benefit payments. The Secretary of Agriculture was to make agreements with growers of the enumerated cash crops under which the government was to pay cash in return for acreage temporarily retired from cultivation. (3) By marketing agreements. The Secretary of Agriculture was authorized to enter into marketing agreements with producers, processors, and distributors of agricultural products "so that competitive wastes may be eliminated, trade practices improved, surpluses moved into markets for consumption, and producers' prices raised." Processors and distributors also might be licensed.

The next step was the imposition of the processing tax to be levied on the "first domestic processing of the basic commodity concerned" (the flour millers, meat packers, etc.); the sums obtained from these persons and corporations were to constitute the fund out of which the benefit or rental payments were to be made. To carry out the provisions of the act there was established within the Department of Agriculture the first of the great *ad hoc* agencies of the New Deal, the Agricultural Adjustment Administration. It should be noted at this point that the principle of rental or benefit payments was extended, in April, 1934, to include the growers of beef and dairy cattle, peanuts, rye, barley, flax, and grain sorghum. Also, in May, 1934, Roosevelt signed a bill including sugar beets and sugar cane among the basic commodities under the control of the Agricultural Adjustment Administration and in effect placing the national production of sugar on a quota basis.

The AAA was established at once, its most important functionaries being an Administrator, a Coadministrator (whose office was later abolished), a General Counsel, and an Economic Adviser; George N. Peek was named the first Administrator and was succeeded by Chester C. Davis. Cotton was the first commodity for which an adjustment program was developed. Some of the outstanding facts in the cotton situation were the following: total number of acres of cotton in cultivation in the United States, July 1, 1933, 40,929,000; number of cotton growers who signed adjustment contracts, 1,026,514; acreage taken out of production in 1933 by these, 10,400,000; total number of bales of cotton produced in United States in 1933, 13,177,000; world supply of American cotton, 1932–33, 26,000,000 bales; world supply of American cotton, 1933–34, 24,800,000 bales; total of cash rental payments ($7 to $20 per acre without option; $6 to $12 per acre with option) on land taken out of production in 1933, $122,000,-000. On June 23 the first contract was signed and on July 12 the campaign was closed; the effort was unusually successful, fully 73 per cent of the total acreage in cultivation in 1933 being signed up. Funds with which to pay the rental or benefit payments came from a processing tax of 4.2 cents a pound net weight on all cotton entering domestic consumption, effective August 1, 1933. According to the report of the AAA, the scheme resulted in an increase of gross farm income of the cotton growers of 100 per cent, for the farm value of the 1932 crop (seed and lint) had been $425,488,-000, while the farm value of the 1933 crop (seed, lint, cash rental

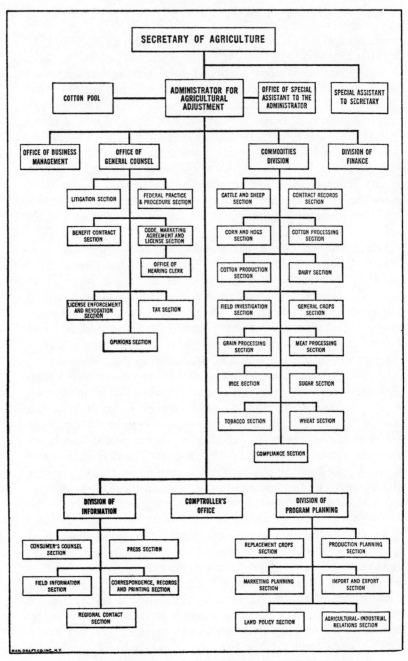

THE AGRICULTURAL ADJUSTMENT ADMINISTRATION

payments, profits on options) was $857,248,000. Prices received by producers averaged 9.5 cents for the 1933 crop, compared with 5.4 cents per pound in December, 1932.

Wheat was the next crop for which a program was developed. On June 20, 1933, the Secretary of Agriculture announced that production adjustment payments would be made to wheat growers on the following basis: payments to be made annually on the 1933, 1934, and 1935 wheat crops to producers entering into contracts to reduce their wheat acreages for 1934 and 1935; payments for the 1933–34 marketing year to amount to 28 cents per bushel on that portion of each producer's base production corresponding to the portion of the total national production which is ordinarily consumed domestically (this was found to be approximately 54 per cent); the contracting producer to agree to reduce his wheat acreage by not more than 20 per cent of his average acreage for the three-year base period, and "to sow in a workmanlike manner an acreage sufficient to produce, under normal yield, the amount in bushels allotted to him."

To protect the American wheat growers from the chances of the world market, in the summer of 1933 the American government sought to enter into an agreement with the principal wheat growing and consuming countries for the purpose of cutting acreage and regulating wheat importations on an international basis. Such an agreement was signed August 25, 1933, and provided that the exporting countries should take definite steps to control their production of exports, while the importing countries were to make efforts to increase wheat consumption and to lower the trade and tariff barriers against its importation. The United States pledged itself to cut acreage 15 per cent of that of the base period 1930–31 to 1932–33. Thus, the acreage reduction plan of the AAA and the world wheat agreement made possible the hope that American wheat farmers would be protected from the catastrophic piling up of wheat surpluses with the consequent depressing of prices.[1]

---

[1] The conclusion of the world wheat agreement was quite unhappy. In the first place, the United States succeeded in cutting acreage not much more than half of the guaranteed 15 per cent; in the second place, Argentina, dissatisfied with its export quota and overburdened by its great surplus, demanded a larger quota than had been originally granted. When this was refused, Argentina's representatives declined, in May, 1934, to sign an international agreement, fixing minimum wheat prices. This action wrecked the conference and made negligible the chances of world valorization of wheat.

The following outstanding facts in the wheat situation indicate how the program worked out: number of wheat growers who signed applications for 1933–34 adjustment contracts, 550,000; total average acreage planted to wheat by all United States farmers for base years 1930 to 1932 inclusive, 65,958,000; total average acreage planted to wheat by contracting producers in base years 1930–32, 50,600,000; acreage removed from production, as pledged in contracts, 7,595,000; estimated net receipts from processing tax of 30 cents per bushel during 1933–34 marketing year, $108,000,000; total benefit payments made to contracting producers in 1933–34 marketing year, $95,000,000; estimated income from 1933–34 wheat crop, including benefit payments, $376,-000,000; income from 1932–33 wheat crop, $169,000,000. The average farm price for the 1932–33 marketing year was 38.6 cents a bushel; the 1933–34 farm price was estimated at 74.1 cents a bushel.

Somewhat different arrangements were made with tobacco and corn and hog growers. In the case of the corn-hog group an emergency program was entered upon under which the AAA purchased 5,000,000 pigs and brood sows (many of which it had to destroy); it also made loans to corn growers for corn properly warehoused and sealed. Subsequently, the corn-hog program was declared effective as of November 5, 1933. The tax on corn was announced as 5 cents per bushel of 56 pounds. For hogs, the taxes were: effective November 5, 50 cents per 100 pounds live weight; December 1, $1; February 1, 1934, $1.50; March 1, 1934, $2.25. The tax on leaf tobacco, effective October 1, was to be 1.7 cents per pound for Maryland tobacco and an approximate average of 3 cents per pound for tobacco from other states. No comprehensive arrangement was worked out in the case of dairy products and for more than a year after the creation of the AAA efforts to formulate a program satisfactory to both producers and consumers were to meet with failure. By the end of June, 1934, the Department had succeeded in drawing up some forty marketing agreements with and in granting licenses to the following agricultural groups and industries in the specified regions, among others: importing alcoholic beverages; bee shippers; celery, Florida; dates, California; citrus fruit, California; citrus fruit, Texas; deciduous fruit, California; deciduous fruit, Northwest; dry skim and evaporated milk; fluid milk (licenses only) for twenty-nine cities; canned olives, California, etc., etc.[2]

The second part of the farm program had to do with the relief of the credit situation. The Agricultural Adjustment Act carried a number of amendments to the Federal Farm Loan Act which provided for the issuance of $2,000,000,000 worth of farm-loan bonds at 4 per cent, only the interest of which was to be guaranteed by the United States government. The Federal Land Banks were to refinance farm mortgages by either purchasing or exchanging the new farm-loan bonds for first mortgages on farm lands. The maximum price these agencies were permitted to pay for such instruments was 50 per cent of the normal value of the land and 20 per cent of the value of the permanent improvements. Also, on June 16 the President signed the Farm Credit Act whose purpose was the strengthening of the federal machinery dealing with the problem of making short-term and medium-term loans for the production and marketing of agricultural products. New banking and credit agencies were set up, namely, a Central Bank for Coöperatives, twelve regional Banks for Coöperatives, and twelve Production Credit Corporations; the last named, in turn, were to control the activities of local Production Credit Associations. By executive order all the government's agricultural credit agencies had been consolidated in a new Farm Credit Administration.

The relief of the farm mortgage situation, the chief purpose of the new legislation, moved slowly. Something of the size of the problem confronting the Farm Credit Administration may be gained from the following. On May 12, 1933, after seventeen years of operation, the Federal Land Banks had outstanding $1,100,000,000 of mortgage loans. In the year preceding May 12, 1933, the twelve Federal Land Banks had closed 7,208 loans totaling $27,000,000. On the other hand, in the five and one-half months immediately following the passage of the Agricultural Adjustment Act (May 12–December 1, 1933), the FCA was in receipt of 433,037 farm loan applications, totaling $1,724,363,809.

[2] In June, 1934, the legality of the whole marketing agreement and licensing machinery of the AAA was challenged when a federal judge at Chicago issued a temporary injunction restraining the Administration from enforcing its milk license agreement in the area.

The difficulty of appraising quickly the farms and improvements prevented any real progress being made to relieve farmers oppressed by onerous mortgage burdens; the result was that in the initial five and one-half months of operations only $145,000,000 had actually been extended to farmers in the form of mortgage loans. Also, the failure of the legislation in the beginning to guarantee principal along with the interest of the new bonds (although this was subsequently corrected) stood in the way of the refinancing of farm mortgages on a wholesale scale.

It was to correct these various inadequacies that Congress, fearing a filibuster by agrarian spokesmen in the closing days of its last session, passed the Frazier-Lemke Farm Bankruptcy bill; the measure was signed by the President with considerable reluctance on June 28, 1934. The purpose of the law was to facilitate agreements between distressed farmers and their creditors and to grant extensions of time to the former during which they might remain in possession of their farms. The act provided that farmers dissatisfied with settlements might ask for appraisals of their property, which were to be "fair and reasonable, though not necessarily the market value"; methods were then set up by which the farmer could repurchase his property at the appraised value with small yearly payments of principal over six years and with interest at 1 per cent. If the creditor or mortgagee objected to this form of settlement the farmer was to be permitted to retain possession under a "reasonable" rental for five years, during which time all bankruptcy proceedings were to be in abeyance. This was the only step taken by the Administration to cope directly with the nation's debt problem, by scaling down a significant portion of it. It remained to be seen whether the same method would be applied to other forms of private debt.

CODES OF FAIR COMPETITION FOR INDUSTRY AND THE RIGHT TO ORGANIZE FOR LABOR

Just as agriculture was to be revived by the application of the just price (in this case a return to the price situation prevailing during the immediate prewar years), so industry and labor were to be saved by the same rule (in the case of industry a return to the price situation of 1926 being the objective, in the case of labor reëmployment as a result of shorter hours and minimum wages).

The New Deal was not prepared to guarantee directly to every large enterpriser and every rentier a fair return on his investment; but it moved toward this goal just the same if somewhat circuitously. Industry, which to some extent had been checked from assuming inevitable monopoly characteristics because of the existence of the anti-trust laws, was now to be formed into cartels and, working through the agencies of its own trade associations, was to devise "codes of fair competition" for the purpose of regulating methods of manufacture, promotion, and sales.

These codes were to have another purpose as well: not only were they to protect industry from its own baser instincts but they were to provide further opportunities for the employment of labor through the establishment of basic maximum working hours and minimum wages and the elimination of child labor. The purchasing power of the working class was to be restored by increasing the total number of persons in industry and by raising the per capita wage of sweated workers to a subsistence level. While there was some talk of providing formally for the leveling upward of all wages so that the stipulated minimum rates would not in effect become the maximums, this idea on a wholesale scale was soon abandoned.

To effectuate these ends Congress passed and the President signed on June 16, 1933, the National Industrial Recovery Act. The Act had three parts, or titles: the first was concerned with the organization of industry and was to remain in force but two years; the second had to do with the creation of a public works program; the third called for the amendment of the Emergency Relief and Construction Act (passed under the Hoover Administration) and included provision for a number of miscellaneous activities. The first section of the first title indicated the character of the far-reaching reforms the New Deal was seeking to inaugurate.

A national emergency productive of widespread unemployment and disorganization of industry, which burdens interstate and foreign commerce, affects the public welfare, and undermines the standards of living of the American people, is hereby declared to exist. It is hereby declared to be the policy of Congress to remove obstructions to the free flow of interstate and foreign commerce which tend to diminish the amount thereof; and to provide for the general welfare by promoting the organization of industry for the purpose of coöperative action among trade groups, to induce and maintain united action of labor and management under adequate governmental sanctions and supervision, to eliminate unfair competitive practices, to promote the fullest possible utilization of the present productive capacity of industries, to avoid undue restrictions of production (except as may be temporarily required), to increase the consumption of industrial and agricultural products by increasing purchasing power, to reduce and relieve unemployment, to improve standards of labor, and otherwise to rehabilitate industry and to conserve natural resources.

The important provisions of the new law were as follows: (1) The President was to establish an agency to which was to be delegated the powers and functions indicated in the act. (2) Codes of fair competition might be drawn up by trade or industrial associations and submitted to the President for his approval. The President was given the power to approve such codes if the associations were "truly representative" of their industries and if the codes were "not designed to promote monopolies or to eliminate or oppress small enterprises." (3) Once such codes were approved, they were enforceable by law; the courts could issue injunctions against violation on the institution of equity proceedings by the United States district attorneys. (4) The President might prescribe codes for industries if none as submitted was approved by him. (5) The President might make agreements or approve voluntary agreements to further the purpose of the law. He was also empowered to institute a licensing system in any industry if that was necessary to make a code or agreement effective. In such cases, no persons could engage in the industries in question without licenses, and licenses were revocable by the President. (This last power was granted for a single year.) (6) Any action under provisions of the law was exempt from the anti-trust acts. (7) Every code of fair competition was to contain the following conditions affecting labor. This was the much discussed section 7 (a) of the law and it is quoted in full.

(1) That employees shall have the right to organize and bargain collectively through representatives of their own choosing, and shall be free from the interference, restraint, or coercion of employers of labor, or their agents, in the designation of such representatives or in self-organization or in other concerted activities for the purpose of collective bargaining or other mutual aid or protection; (2) that no employee and no one seeking employment shall be required as a condition of em-

ployment to join any company union or to refrain from joining, organizing, or assisting a labor organization of his own choosing; and (3) that employers shall comply with the maximum hours of labor, minimum rates of pay, and other conditions of employment approved or prescribed by the President.

Thus, industry could unite in its own trade groups for purposes of eliminating methods of unfair competition and in this way arrive at a just price for the use of its capital and for the commodities it fabricated and sold; the workers similarly could unite in their own trade unions and by all the methods of collective bargaining available to them compel the payment of a just price for their labor.

The National Recovery Administration was the agency created to supervise the preparation of codes and enforce their observance; and Gen. Hugh S. Johnson was named the first Administrator. The chief assistants of the Administrator were an Assistant Administrator for Industry, an Assistant Administrator for Labor, a Special Assistant Administrator, the General Counsel, and the Economic Adviser. There were also eight division administrators in charge of the codes themselves, a compliance board (in charge of enforcement), and advisory boards for industry, labor, and consumers. The Industrial Advisory Board, composed of active business men who rotated in office and served in Washington for limited periods, advised the Administrator and his assistants on all matters of industrial policy. The Consumers' Advisory Board was established to represent the interests and viewpoints of consumers and to advise the Administrator and his assistants how the provisions of proposed codes affected prices to consumers and standards of quality. The Labor Advisory Board was to advise the Administrator and his assistants on labor questions, especially hours, wages, and working conditions. This board had as its objectives the elimination of child labor, the establishment of shorter hours and higher wages, the protection of the right of labor to collective bargaining, the appointment of a representative of labor to each of the code or enforcement authorities, and the creation within industries of committees on labeling and standards.

To protect the rights of labor and to settle by mediation, conciliation, or arbitration all industrial disputes the National Labor Board was created on August 5, 1933. It was headed by Senator

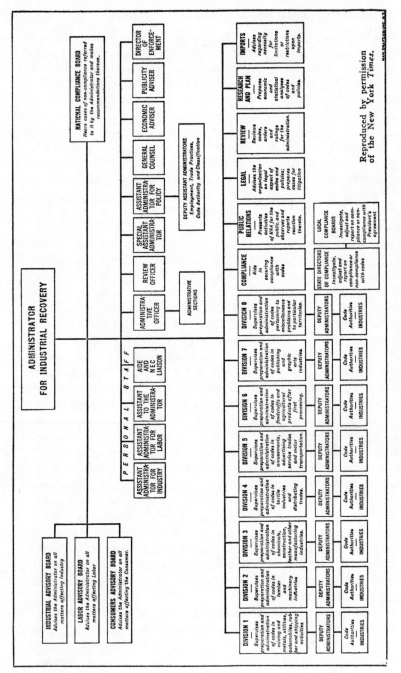

THE NATIONAL RECOVERY ADMINISTRATION

Robert F. Wagner and was made up of twelve additional persons, six of whom represented the employers and the other six the workers. The Board was empowered to establish local or regional boards, upon which employers and workers also were to have equal representation, supervise elections in industrial plants where the workers were to choose their own representatives for their negotiations with employers, and refer its findings of violation of section 7 (a) of the NIRA to the Attorney General and to the Compliance Division of the NRA.

The following was the Board's own statement of principles:

(a) Recognition that employees shall have the right to organize and bargain collectively through representatives of their own choosing and shall be free from the interference, restraint, or coercion of employers of labor or their agents in the designation of such representatives or in self-organization or in other concerted activities for the purpose of collective bargaining or other mutual aid or protection.

(b) Recognition that no employee, or anyone seeking employment, shall be required as a condition of employment to join any company union or to refrain from joining, organizing, or assisting a labor organization of his own choosing.

(c) Recognition that every opportunity should be afforded to employers and employees in any trade or industry where collective bargaining prevails to establish by mutual agreement the standards as to the maximum hours of labor, minimum rates of pay, and other conditions of employment.

(d) Recognition that those standards shall not be lower than those sanctioned by the President in accordance with the provisions of the NIRA.

The code-making process in most cases was comparatively simple. Representative groups in each industry, usually working through their trade associations (and therefore without labor representation), drew up codes which were presented to the NRA for consideration. Public hearings were then held under the direction of deputy administrators, at which the viewpoints and objections of consumers, labor, and other interested parties could be presented; upon the acceptance of these codes by the deputy and division administrators the documents were submitted to the President or the NRA Administrator for his approval. (The NRA Administrator had been authorized by the President to approve codes for industries employing 50,000 or fewer workers.) After proper approval a code had the force of a statute. With the completion of the code, an agency was set up in each industry called the Code Authority which was, in effect, the agency of self-government in the industry. In most cases the Code Authorities were merely the old trade associations in new guise, except for the occasional addition of a small number of "public" representatives; labor as such was given a formal place on very few of the Code Authorities.

Compliance with the codes of fair competition and with the President's Reëmployment Agreement (described below) was obtained by the Compliance Division with the assistance of a nation-wide system of local NRA Compliance Boards and state adjustment agencies. In the event of the Compliance Division's inability to gain enforcement, the case was referred to the National Compliance Board; this agency could undertake further efforts at an adjustment of the complaint and, if necessary, recommend action by the Attorney General or the Federal Trade Commission. The Compliance Division had jurisdiction over all complaints of violation of codes and of the President's Reëmployment Agreement except those involving labor disputes and the right of employees to bargain collectively. These labor disputes were handled, as has been pointed out, by the National Labor Board and the Regional Labor Boards or other agencies set up under its authority.

Because of the slowness attending the preparation of the codes it was decided to draw up a blanket code, called the President's Reëmployment Agreement, which was to be effective from September 1 to December 31, 1933 for all employers voluntarily signing it. Subsequently, the President offered to extend the agreement with every employer not yet covered by a code for his particular industry for a further four-months period. The blanket code provided, as regards clerical workers, a 40-hour week with minimum wages from $12 to $15 a week; and as regards industrial workers, a 35-hour week with minimum wages from 30 cents to 40 cents an hour. Children below 16 years were not to be employed except that between the ages of 14 years and 16 years children might be employed in all activities (but not in manufacturing or mechanical industries) for three hours a day between 7 A. M. and 7 P. M. All signers of the blanket code were to receive Blue Eagles, the emblem which indicated compliance with the spirit of the National

Industrial Recovery Act; the Blue Eagle also could be displayed by employers for whose industries codes had already been drawn up and accepted, since such acceptance automatically put every employer in the particular industry under the aegis of the NRA and all its machinery.

The first code to be signed was the cotton textile code, this receiving the President's approval July 9; on July 26, the wool textile and shipbuilding codes were approved; on August 4, the electrical and coat and suit codes; on August 19, the petroleum, iron and steel, and lumber codes. By the middle of May, 1934, more than 400 codes had been prepared and signed while an additional 300 codes already had had their hearings completed. A year after the establishment of the NRA it was estimated that some 20,000,000 workers were employed under the Blue Eagle.

The cotton textile code presaged the general character of the arrangements that were going to be drawn up. The labor provisions were the following: children under 16 years of age were to be denied employment in the mills of the industry; the minimum wage (except for learners for a six-week period, cleaners, and outside employees) was to be $13 a week in the North and $12 a week in the South; the working week was to be 40 hours long; speeding-up of work (the stretch-out) was prohibited. The following production and price-controlling devices were written into the code: machinery was not to be operated more than 80 hours a week; for the installation of new machinery by persons engaged or engaging in the industry (except for replacements), certificates had to be obtained from the Administration; the listing of future prices (the so-called open-price arrangement) and control over "methods and conditions of trading" were part of the functions delegated to the Code Authority.

As far as labor was concerned, the standards set up in the cotton textile code were not deviated from very markedly thereafter; indeed, up to the end of January, 1934, only 15 out of 234 codes provided for less than the 40-hour week.[3] Minimum wages ranged in the great majority of cases between $12 and $15, while the

[3] In May, 1934, in a statement made by the Labor Advisory Board, this interesting situation was pointed out: "The present codes are supposed to have secured a 40-hour week, but actually so many groups are excepted (some 2,000 groups in the first 400 codes), and so many exemptions have been permitted for seasonality, emergencies, averaging periods, tolerances, etc. that the 40-hour week of scheduled production still remains to be achieved."

labor of children under 16 years was banned. Industry, however, displayed extraordinary ingenuity in devising methods for limiting production and controlling prices, that is to say, inaugurating monopoly practices. In fact, more than one-half of the codes accepted by May, 1934, contained price-fixing and output limitation features. These were usually of seven kinds: (1) the establishment of minimum prices, or the maintenance of resale prices; (2) the fixing of a minimum mark-up (as in the retail code); (3) the prohibition of the sale of commodities below the cost of production; (4) the creation of open-price posting arrangements (Under this method, there were filed with the Code Authority schedules of prices, discounts, and terms of sale under which the companies were doing business. Until such schedules were revised after a period of notice, members of the industry were forbidden to make changes in prices or terms. In effect, therefore, because pressure could be brought on companies whose practices were radically out of line, open-price arrangements meant the establishment of uniform prices.); (5) multiple basing-point systems (as in steel); (6) the fixing of prices under governmental control (as in coal and oil); (7) the limitation of production (The usual methods were by the allotment of production quotas to individual units in the industry, by prohibitions against the increase of productive capacity, and by a uniform limitation on machine hours.).[4] Another characteristic which led to the same tendency of monopoly control was the arbitrary definition of "cost," particularly in determining the fixing of minimum prices. Some codes defined cost as an average for the industry, others as a combination of the average cost and that of the individual concern, others as the individual's alone or the individual's cost plus a labor allowance, and still others as the cost of the lowest "representative member" of the industry. Finally, the codes set out to make sales practices uniform in order to check the taking of unfair advantages among competitors. This group of provisions usually applied to such matters as cash discounts, dis-

[4] Thirty-six out of the first 280 codes contained restrictions on the installation of new machinery, on increase in productive plant capacity, or on hours of operation of machines. Limitation on the use of new machinery fell into four classes: a direct prohibition against the extension of capacity (steel code); the requirement of authorization for an extension of capacity (119 codes, including cotton textile, transit, ice); extensions were to be recommended by the Code Authority in question (18 codes, including hosiery, limestone, cotton garments); restrictions by agreement (motor vehicle storage and parking code).

counts to jobbers and wholesalers, standardization of products, the kind of advisory services to be rendered customers, limitations on guarantees, methods of allowing credit, defamation of rivals' goods, and the like.

By the middle of July, 1934, some 476 codes, covering 90 per cent of the nation's industry, had been drawn up. To facilitate quick compliance on the part of the remaining industries, most of which were of minor significance, the Administrator drew up a "basic code" to which he invited acceptance. As an alternative he offered business men the right to subscribe to the existing codes of industries resembling their own. The basic code, in line with the position that the NRA was compelled to take, did not permit price-fixing; prices merely could be filed with "a confidential and disinterested person," there was to be no waiting period, and minimum prices could be fixed by the code administrator only when an emergency was declared to exist. While the code did not specify maximum hours and minimum wages (these were to be established in particular cases on the basis of the rates carried in codes governing related industries), it did provide for adjustments in the whole wage scale in order to continue to maintain the differentials existing between the minimum and the other levels.

While, within the first year of the New Deal's existence, no test case was brought up to the highest tribunal of the land so that there still continued to exist some doubt as to whether the Supreme Court would regard the whole NRA machinery as constitutional, evidences were early afforded of the probable attitude of the Court. In January, 1934, by a vote of five to four, the court sustained the Minnesota Mortgage Moratorium Act under which, for a period of two years, the state suspended contracts concerning title to real estate sold under mortgage foreclosures. Chief Justice Hughes in writing the majority opinion (in which he was joined by Justices Roberts, Stone, Brandeis, and Cardozo), defended the legislation because of the existence of urgent public need; in fact, the Minnesota law was designed not for the protection of the individual but "for the protection of a basic interest of society." Said the Chief Justice:

Where in earlier days it was thought that only concerns of the individuals or classes were involved and that those of the state itself were touched only remotely, it has later been found that the fundamental interests of the state are directly affected, and that the question is no longer merely that of one party against another but of the use of reasonable means to safeguard the economic structure upon which the good of all depends.

And in March of the same year, by the same vote of five to four with the same justices participating in the majority opinion, the Court upheld a law of New York state which sought to fix the price of milk. It was plain that the Supreme Court, on the grounds of the existence of a national emergency, was inclined to regard with favor legislation which normally would have been considered as in violation of the Fourteenth Amendment; but, of course, it was impossible to foretell, in view of the closeness of the early decisions, what the Court's stand would be on questions arising out of the enforcement of the NIRA and the codes formulated under it. The Roosevelt Administration showed no desire to force a test and was proceeding on the assumption that all its acts were in scrupulous observance of the rights of the individual.

RECOVERY BY PUBLIC WORKS

It has been pointed out above that the second title of the NIRA provided for the establishment of a federal public works program as another device for starting the wheels of industry going once more and thus aiding recovery. The law created a fund of $3,300,-000,000 for this purpose and set up the Federal Emergency Administration of Public Works (PWA) to administer it. Secretary of Interior Ickes was named the first Administrator. Section 202 of the law authorized the Administrator, under the direction of the President, to prepare a program which was to include, among other things, the following: (1) the construction, repair, and improvement of public highways and parkways, public buildings, and any publicly owned instrumentalities and facilities; (2) the conservation and development of natural resources, including control, utilization, and purification of waters, prevention of soil erosion, development of water power, transmission of electrical energy, and the construction of river and harbor improvements and flood control; (3) any projects of a character heretofore constructed or carried on either directly by public authority or with public aid to serve the interests of the general public; (4) the

construction, reconstruction, alteration, or repair under public regulation or control of low-cost housing and slum-clearance projects;
(5) any project of any character heretofore eligible for loans
under the provisions of the Emergency Relief and Construction
Act of 1932. This last was to include loans for the construction or
completion of hospitals the operation of which was partly financed
from public funds, the construction of naval vessels under the
terms or limits of the London Naval Limitation Treaty of 1930,
aircraft required for this purpose, as well as army housing and the
mechanization or motorization of army equipment.

While a detailed plan for public works was being drawn up,
the President was authorized and empowered, through the Administrator or through such other agencies as he might designate
or create: (1) to construct, finance, or aid in the construction or
financing of any public work projects included in the comprehensive plan referred to above; (2) to make grants to states,
municipalities, or other public bodies upon such terms as he, the
President, might prescribe, for the construction, repair or improvement of any projects included in the enumeration in the preceding
paragraph, but no such grant should be in excess of 30 per cent of
the cost of the labor and the materials employed upon such projects; (3) to acquire by purchase or the power of eminent domain
any real or personal property in connection with the construction
of any such project; (4) to aid in the financing of such railroad
maintenance and equipment as may be approved by the Interstate
Commerce Commission; (5) to advance the unappropriated
balance of the sum authorized by the construction and equipment
of an annex to the Library of Congress.

Because of restrictions with which the Administrator ringed
around the public works program, it made slow progress and it is
doubtful whether the scheme lived up to the expectations of its
supporters that it would prime the industrial pump. The policies
worked out by the PWA to guide its program included: (1) Every
project must be socially desirable and qualified on the basis of a
careful economic, engineering, financial, and legal examination.
(2) Repayment of loans was expected and reasonable security was
required. (3) The PWA would observe all legal restrictions on
local bodies assuming debts. (4) It would not encourage localities
to become "hopelessly bankrupt." (5) Projects were to be for the

public welfare and not for private profit. (6) Every misuse of public money would be regarded as a betrayal of a public trust and moved against vigorously by the PWA.

Within a single year, that is, by June 16, 1934, the PWA had allotted its entire $3,300,000,000 fund to 13,266 federal projects and 2,407 non-federal projects. It is to be noted that the fund was frequently dipped into by Congress for various emergency purposes so that many of the allotments could not be regarded strictly as of a public works character, that is to say, they could not succeed in stimulating private industrial activity on a very large scale. In all, approximately one-third of the fund was allotted by Congressional enactment or executive order. Of the remainder, about $1,400,000,000 went to federal construction projects throughout the country and a little under $1,000,000,000 went for loans, loans plus grants, or grants alone to various local governments or for construction in the public interest. However, not much more than $1,200,000,000 was actually disbursed in the first year of the PWA's existence; and the Administrator himself estimated that only about $500,000,000 would be paid out during 1935. As an example of how slowly the fund moved, it may be noted that by April 30, 1934, the Navy, which had been allotted $238,000,000 for the building of warships, had spent but $21,-400,000; and the Army, which had been allotted $103,000,000 for military posts and housing, improvement of seacoast defenses, motorization, and airplanes, had spent but $20,000,000; while private railroad companies, which had been allotted $200,000,000 as work-creating loans, had spent $43,590,000. The most important allotments and allocations were as follows: loans and grants to states, cities, counties, railroad companies, and others for non-federal projects, $759,550,000; federal aid road system construction by states, $400,000,000; Civil Works Administration, $400,-000,000; Civilian Conservation Camps, $323,000,000; Emergency Housing Corporation of PWA, $127,565,000; Farm Credit Administration, $100,000,000; Tennessee Valley Authority, $50,000,-000; Surplus Relief Corporation, $25,000,000; power and reclamation projects being constructed by Reclamation Bureau, $103,535,000; subsistence homesteads, $25,000,000; public buildings, $67,427,000; flood control, $73,921,000; general river and harbor work, $179,924,000; miscellaneous allotments to bureaus and departments of the federal government, $146,292,000. The smallness of the allotment for housing, which was one of the great hopes for the PWA, will be noted. In the beginning, enthusiasts looked for an organized public attack on slums and the erection of vast numbers of dwellings for families with low incomes. At the end of a year Secretary Ickes confessed that the housing program, "because of restrictive land and property laws, . . . must necessarily be a slow and steady development instead of one of swift function."

III. THE NEW DEAL IN THEORY: SAVING THE CREDIT STRUCTURE AND REGAINING FOREIGN MARKETS

DEVALUING THE DOLLAR AS A RELIEF MEASURE

THE drive to raise prices and relieve the pressure of the debt burden soon turned the thoughts of the Administration to the problem of currency expansion. Immediately, it became obvious that some form of inflation was necessary; the hope was, of course, that it could be controlled. The currency policy of the New Deal may be summed up simply: it revolved about the effort to check deflation without resorting to fiat mcney pure and simple.

Preliminary steps indicated that the United States was soon destined to go off the gold standard, along with most of the outstanding nations of the world. On March 10, 1933, the President issued an executive order to halt the export of gold except when licensed by the Treasury; on April 5, the hoarding of gold coin, gold bullion, and gold certificates was forbidden; and on April 19, the United States formally departed from the gold standard when an executive order stopped the free movement of the metal. The document declared that the earmarking for foreign account and the export of gold, gold bullion, and gold certificates from the United States was prohibited, the Secretary of the Treasury being permitted to issue licenses only in the case of a number of excepted instances; also, the Secretary of the Treasury was authorized to investigate, regulate, or prohibit any transactions in foreign exchange and the export or withdrawal of currency from the United States. To achieve the same result in a somewhat different way the Gold Repeal Joint Resolution, approved June 5, 1933, canceled the gold clause in all federal and private obligations and made contracts and debts payable in legal tender.

The Agricultural Adjustment Act of May 12, 1933 embodied the first positive efforts to increase the amount of money in circulation. It should be noted, however, that the Administration in this law won its initial battle to prevent inflation by statutory order, for the act did not require the President to carry out its terms but merely authorized him to do so "in his discretion." He could undertake one or all of the following in order to expand credit: (1) Require the Federal Reserve Banks to conduct open-market operations in United States securities up to the value of $3,000,-000,000. (2) Issue up to $3,000,000,000 worth of United States notes. This paper currency could be used by the government only in retiring outstanding federal obligations but, of course, it was to be legal tender for all public and private debts. (3) Reduce the gold content of the dollar as much as 50 per cent; and set up a bimetallic system and provide for the unlimited coinage of both gold and silver at ratios fixed by him. (4) Accept, for a period of six months, silver from foreign governments in payment of their indebtedness to the United States, at a price of not more than 50 cents an ounce. However, not more than $200,000,000 worth of silver was to be taken on the account of the intergovernmental debts.

Whether due to these measures, a reawakening of general confidence, or in anticipation of higher costs because of the expected enactment of the AAA and the NIRA, it is not necessary to decide: it is enough to note that the value of the dollar began to drop in the middle of April, that prices began to mount and that, in fact, they continued to do so until the middle of July. The expectation that the country could pull itself out of its difficulties without the necessity for concern over the stabilization of the world monetary situation helps to explain our indifference to international currents—and the collapse of the World Economic Conference. The conference resolved itself into a struggle between nationalist and internationalist objectives, between world stabilization of currency and national valuation, and nationalism won. After having led the powers to believe that relief to the world price level could come only by concerted action, Mr. Roosevelt dramatically changed his mind while the conferees were in session and in effect repudiated his own delegation: we were to go our own way as regards monetary program and price schemes.

The preliminaries of the conference were indeed spectacular. The leading powers of the globe were invited to send representatives to Washington for the purpose of engaging in bilateral conversations with the President and preparing the agenda; and Great Britain, France, Italy, Germany, Japan, China, Argentina, Brazil,

Chile, Mexico, and Canada responded, beginning with the appearance at Washington on April 21 of Great Britain's Prime Minister Ramsay MacDonald. When the American delegation, headed by Secretary of State Hull, left for London, the seat of the conference, early in June, it was generally felt that a program had been agreed to which centered in "the eventual restoration of a revised international gold standard." In the words of Ernest K. Lindley: "The American monetary formula . . . proposed a reduction in the gold cover of currencies and the optional use of silver as part coverage. . . . Other main points in the American program were: synchronizing of public works programs, control of production of basic commodities, elimination of extreme trade barriers and a beginning in the reduction of tariffs, the raising and stabilization of the price of silver between 50 and 75 cents an ounce."

The conference opened on June 12 and broke up July 27 without having reached any understanding either on currency stabilization or on price-raising devices or on tariff reduction; what achievements it had to its credit—as to increasing the price of silver and wheat valorization—were slight and indeed subsequently proved to be entirely negligible. The insistence of European delegations, particularly the French, upon considering at the beginning the problem of currency stabilization, despite Secretary Hull's desire to effect first a world tariff-reduction agreement, prompted the President to send to London Assistant Secretary of State Moley with new instructions: the American representatives were by no means to accept stabilization of the dollar or promise the renewal of gold shipments. All he would accede to was a willingness (in Mr. Lindley's words): "to let central banks coöperate in 'studying' exchange fluctuations and eliminating speculative activities centering in London, Paris, Amsterdam, and Brussels." The countersuggestion of the gold countries and Great Britain that the President join them in a declaration favoring a return to the gold standard as soon as possible met with an immediate and tart rejection. On July 3, from the U.S.S. *Indianapolis,* cruising off the Atlantic coast, the President cabled the conference that he would consider it "a catastrophe amounting to a world tragedy," if the body allowed itself to be diverted from its great purposes by "the proposal of a purely artificial and temporary experiment affecting the monetary exchange of a few countries only. . . . The sound internal economic system of a nation is a greater factor in its well-being than the price of its currency in changing terms of the currencies of other nations." And as for the United States, it was seeking "the kind of a dollar which, a generation hence, will have the same purchasing and debt-paying power as the dollar value we hope to attain in the near future." Thus the President had chosen the nationalist path of self-sufficiency as against recovery by world agreement and the revitalization once more of international trade and the free flow of credits; in the face of this decision the conference had no choice but to adjourn *sine die*.

But following the early summer's rise, prices began to slip once more, and again the value of the dollar became a leading Administration concern. Farm prices, in particular, declined, and this exactly at the period when the new crops were ready for the market. Farm strikes, accompanied by violence, broke out in seven western states; the governor of North Dakota placed an embargo on the shipment of wheat, while other executives in the disaffected area seriously considered following his example. To still the growing clamor of the inflationists, the President on October 22 announced a new policy: the government would purchase gold freshly mined in the United States and also (by announcement three days later) foreign gold, at figures to be determined by the RFC; in this way a progressively cheaper value on the dollar would be set. The immediate purposes of the device were "to restore price levels" and "to restore a balance in the price structure so that farmers may exchange their products for the products of industry on a fairer exchange basis"; the ultimate goal was to be the establishment and maintenance of a "dollar which will not change its purchasing and debt-paying power during the succeeding generation."

The RFC at once began buying gold and continued the operation for a number of months; the dollar began to decline in relation to foreign currencies; commodity prices, however, did not rise correspondingly. Thus, between October 25 and November 10, the dollar depreciated 6.8 per cent in foreign exchange, while the price of cotton advanced only 1.6 per cent, the price of wheat advanced only 2 per cent, and the average price of fifty common stocks rose barely three-eighths of 1 per cent. In the two weeks from October 24 to November 6, the general level of wholesale commodity prices actually fell, according to the weekly index of the *Annalist*, from 103.8 to 103. The New York *Times'* comment was pertinent: "The disparity between the fall in the gold value of the dollar and the meager advance in sensitive prices on the speculative commodity and stock exchanges is marked when it is recalled that prices should, in theory, show a percentage of advance greater than the percentages of the fall of the dollar." By the end of 1933 the net depreciation of the dollar, in terms of gold, amounted to 11.4 per cent.

The President's hope of raising prices by devaluing the dollar soon proved illusory. Indeed, it was pointed out to him as early as November 16, 1933, by Professor O. M. W. Sprague, that his confidence for recovery by this method did not have the slightest relation to economic reality. As Professor Sprague said: "But mere depreciation of the currency in relation to the currencies of other countries will not bring about a general rise in prices . . . at a time when there is large excess plant capacity and millions of unemployed wage earners. An advance in prices that has any promise of being maintained requires the development of conditions that will permit a sustained demand for more labor and more materials, with resultant increase in the production of goods and services and a higher standard of living."

Nevertheless, the President persevered in his course. On December 21, acting on the authority given him in the Agricultural Adjustment Act, cited above, Roosevelt ordered the Treasury during the next four years to buy all the silver mined in the United States—coming to approximately 24,000,000 ounces annually—at 64½ cents an ounce. (This was 21½ cents above the market level on the day in question.) On January 15, 1934, he asked Congress to enact a measure which would directly allow dollar devaluation. The new bill was to give the President power: (1) to fix the limits for devaluation of the dollar at from 50 to 60 cents in terms of its old gold content; (2) to authorize him to "manage" the dollar within these limits, by making such changes in its value as he deemed necessary; (3) to impound in the Treasury the vast stocks of gold held by the Federal Reserve Banks; (4) to assure to the government whatever profit might result from an increase in the value of this metal; and (5) to use part of this profit to create a fund of $2,000,000,000 with which to "stabilize" the dollar.

Congress immediately complied, the bill was carried by both houses and signed January 30, and two days later Roosevelt fixed the value of the dollar at 59.06 cents in terms of its old parity. The value of the maneuver, as a price-raising device, stood as follows:

From April 19, 1933, when the gold standard had been abandoned, to May 1, 1934, the wholesale price commodity index of 784 commodities, as compiled by the Department of Labor, rose 22 per cent; in the same period, the gold content of the dollar was reduced 41 per cent. It was inevitable, therefore, that the Administration should yield before the growing pressure of the inflationists, particularly the silverites. After having steadfastly refused to consider various proposals, some of which involved the sale of American agricultural surpluses to foreign countries and the acceptance of payment in silver or silver bullion at a value up to 25 per cent above the world market price of silver, the President capitulated late in May, 1934, and announced that he would give his consent to the enactment of silver legislation.

The President proposed: (1) A new national policy to increase the use of silver in the country's monetary stocks "with the ultimate objective of having and maintaining one-fourth of their monetary value in silver to three-fourths in gold." (2) Authorizing and directing the President to purchase silver to attain this objective ultimately. (3) Authority to buy present accumulations of domestic silver at not more than 50 cents an ounce. (4) Nationalization of silver, as was done with gold, to be permissive, and to be undertaken when in the President's judgment such a course was wise. Then the present surpluses of silver would be taken over and the government would regulate imports, exports, and dealings in monetary silver. (5) A tax of 50 per cent on the profits accruing from dealings in silver. The Silver Purchase Act of 1934, incorporating these provisions, was passed by Congress and approved by Roosevelt on June 19, 1934. It was generally doubted that the addition of silver to the country's monetary reserve would affect prices particularly, since nine-tenths of the country's money was not currency but bank credit. Thus, more than a year after the inauguration of the New Deal currency program, its chief objective, the raising of prices, had not been seriously achieved. Whether unchecked inflation was yet to be the country's lot, it was, however, impossible to foretell in midsummer, 1934.

Credit Expansion

The chief agency for the expansion of credit was the RFC. It has already been pointed out how the RFC had been created by the Hoover Administration in its fight on the depression. The rationale of the agency had been based on the assumption that industrial activity would be revived if governmental funds, in the shape of loans, were made available to release the frozen assets of the financial institutions of the country; in this fashion, the benefits would flow from the top down into the broad base of industrial enterprise. The act establishing the RFC (and its later amendments) therefore called for the granting of loans, secured by collateral, to banks, trust companies, building and loan associations, railroads, insurance companies, mortgage loan companies, federal land banks, joint stock land banks, intermediate credit banks, and agricultural credit corporations. The RFC was also authorized to subscribe to insurance company preferred stock and to make loans upon or purchase the assets of any banking institution closed between December 31, 1929 and January 1, 1934; it could, too, as was mentioned above, subscribe to the preferred stock, capital notes, and debentures of banks and trust companies. The RFC's funds came from the capital of $500,000,000 subscribed by the government and the power of the corporation to issue up to $4,075,000,000 of notes, plus such amounts as might be applied to the purchase of preferred stock, capital notes, and debentures of banks and trust companies.

While the RFC could not make loans directly to industry, eligible borrowers, such as mortgage loan companies, trust companies, and banks, could obtain loans from the RFC for the purpose of relending the proceeds on proper security to private individuals, firms, and corporations engaging in business or industry. Two such classes of loans were acceptable: (1) Loans repayable in six months to be relent to manufacturers and merchants to supply funds for the purchase of materials for manufacture or to cover the actual cost of labor in the manufacture and processing of material. (2) Loans of sound character repayable within three years, where the proceeds were to be used principally for temporary working capital requirements of industrial or mercantile concerns and the need for the loans could be definitely established. The RFC could also make loans to financial institutions which were closed or in process of liquidation.

Between February 2, 1932 and April 30, 1934, the RFC made cash advances totaling $5,139,430,378 of which $1,344,064,992 went to other government agencies and for the relief of destitution, and $3,795,390,387 went to private borrowers. In the latter group, repayments amounting to $1,382,828,921 had been received, leaving a balance outstanding of $2,413,648,170. Banks and trust companies were the largest class of borrowers and to some 7,080 of these institutions loans totaling $1,995,061,938 were authorized. Of this amount $1,552,919,903 had been disbursed in cash and $925,459,565 had been repaid, or 60 per cent. Since the passage of the Emergency Banking Act, the RFC authorized or made agreements to purchase $659,380,000 of preferred stock in 3,278 banks and trust companies, $165,790,000 of capital notes in 183 institutions, and $225,811,050 of debentures in 2,452 institutions. Of these authorized amounts a total of $640,033,292 was actually expended. The RFC authorized loans for the reorganization or liquidation of closed financial institutions aggregating $762,-487,050 to 2,028 institutions; of this amount $491,595,699 had been disbursed, $222,307,370 remained for the credit of the borrowers, and $145,352,593 had been repaid. The table on page 62 indicates the more important loans made and the amounts repaid, as of April 30, 1934. By act approved January 20, 1934, the RFC was continued as a lending body for one year, or until February 1, 1935; after then it was to become only a liquidating corporation.

As another device for the expansion of credit the Loans-to-Industry Act was passed (approved by the President June 19, 1934). This authorized direct loans to business organizations in an amount totaling $580,000,000. No loan was to exceed $500,000. The revolving fund was to be made up of $280,000,000 supplied by Federal Reserve Banks and $300,000,000 by the RFC. The act placed the following limitations on borrowing: (1) the applicant was to have been established in business prior to January 1, 1934; (2) adequate security was to be provided; (3) the maturity of loans was not to exceed five years; (4) the applicant was to be solvent at the time of the disbursement of the loan; (5) credit at prevailing bank rates for loans was not to be otherwise available at banks; (6) loans were to be made only when reasonable assurance of continued or increased employment of labor was offered; (7) the RFC might fix other terms, conditions, and restrictions. The RFC announced that it would make loans primarily to supply working capital as contrasted with fixed capital; also, the following types of security would be acceptable: a first mortgage on real

Class	Loans	Repayments
	(000 omitted)	
Banks and trust companies	$1,552,919	$925,459
Railroads	402,506	57,572
Mortgage loan companies	251,750	63,742
Federal land banks	193,618	—
Regional agricultural credit corp.	170,543	153,825
Building and loan associations	114,132	63,333
Insurance companies	89,326	50,752
Joint stock land banks	15,196	4,578
Livestock credit corporations	12,668	10,949
Federal intermediate credit banks	9,250	9,250
State funds for insurance of public moneys	5,887	3,123
Agricultural credit corporations	5,261	4,352
Credit unions	578	89
To aid in financing self-liquidating construction projects	86,604	3,938
To aid in financing sale of agricultural surpluses in foreign markets	12,851	521
To Commodity Credit Corporation for:		
Loans on cotton	98,995	} 22,715
Loans on corn	86,798	

estate, plant, and equipment, a first mortgage on chattels, an assignment of current accounts or notes receivable, trade acceptances, and warehouse receipts. Compliance with NRA codes was a prerequisite for the filing of applications.

REFORM IN BANKING, SECURITIES, AND EXCHANGES

The New Deal also moved to effect certain permanent reforms in the banking structure of the nation; most of these grew out of inadequacies in banking practice as revealed by the speculative orgy during the boom period, the inability of banks to withstand the rigors of the crisis, and the sensational disclosures of the Senate Committee on Banking and Currency in its investigation of security exchanges and of private banks and bank affiliates engaged in floating securities.[1] These changes were embodied in the Glass-Steagall bill, which was approved June 16, 1933. The important features of this measure were the following: (1) Deposits were to be guaranteed through the creation of an agency known as the Federal Deposit Insurance Corporation, whose capital was to be built up by subscriptions from the federal government, every Federal Reserve Bank, and all banks becoming members of the insurance plan. A temporary scheme was to operate from January 1 to July 1, 1934; thenceforth, the permanent features of the act were in effect. (This was amended in June, 1934, to extend the temporary plan for one year.) They provided that all banks in the Federal Reserve system were members, as were such other banks as also acquired class A stock of the deposit corporation. (Subscriptions to class A stock were to be in an amount equal to one-half of 1 per cent of the bank's total deposit liabilities; this was to be a dividend stock, and banks owning it were to be subject to assessment on their deposit liability to replace losses.) The deposits of these banks were to be insured for 100 per cent of all deposits up to $10,000, for 75 per cent of deposits from $10,000 to $50,000, and for 50 per cent of deposits over $50,000. No bank could remain a member of the deposit corporation after July 1, 1936 (amended to July 1, 1937) unless it became a member of the Federal Reserve system. It may be pointed out here that of the 16,751 banks in the country, 13,423 banks insured their deposits with the Federal Deposit Insurance Corporation as of January 1, 1934; 7,372 of these did not belong to the Federal Reserve system.

(2) A new plan was devised for handling failed banks under which the deposit corporation was to be appointed receiver in the case of all national banks and for those state banks where the state law permitted and the state officials gave their consent. The deposit corporation was then to turn over the sums due to depositors not to them directly but to a new national bank especially created.

(3) Within a year, member banks were to be divorced from their security affiliates; also, private bankers were to choose between doing an investment and a deposit business. The first meant

---

[1] This investigation was begun in April, 1932, and as a result of the support of President Roosevelt continued into 1934. Under the able direction of Ferdinand Pecora as counsel its revelations were as significant as those of the famous Pujo Committee investigation of the Money Trust in 1912.

that banks for deposit could not also have associated with them corporations whose business it was to promote security issues. The second provision implied that great banking houses like J. P. Morgan and Co., Kuhn, Loeb and Co., and the National City Company (an affiliate of the National City Bank) could no longer float security issues and act as the depositories of great corporations at the same time.

(4) National banks might have branches anywhere within a state, if the state law permitted state banks to do so. (5) In an effort to check excessive speculative activity, the Federal Reserve Board was given the power to deny the credit facilities of the system to banks lending too much money for speculation in securities, real estate or commodities. (6) Executive officers of Federal Reserve Banks were to be prohibited from borrowing from their own banks. (7) Membership in the Federal Reserve system was widened to include industrial banks and savings banks. (8) Payment of interest on demand deposits by member banks was forbidden.

Also, to protect the purchasers of securities, Congress passed and the President signed on May 27, 1933, the Federal Securities Act. Except in the case of certain exempt securities and transactions (federal, state, and municipal bonds; short-time commercial paper; securities of educational, religious, and charitable institutions; those of building and loan associations; securities of railroads), no new securities were to be offered in interstate commerce publicly or through the mails unless such issues were first sworn to and registered with the Federal Trade Commission. (By subsequent amendment the supervisory duties were placed in the hands of a new commission, the Securities and Exchange Commission.) Such sworn statements were to include, among other things: all commissions or discounts paid or to be paid by the issuer to the underwriter; a full description of all factors surrounding the physical issuance of the securities; names of directors and officers of the issuing company; names of holders of 10 per cent or more of prior securities issued by the company; and a detailed description of the business and financial condition of the company and the salaries of its officers. If the registration form contained an untrue statement of a material fact or omitted a material fact, the issuing corporation, its officers and directors, and the underwriters participating in the issue's sale were to be liable and purchasers of the security could sue to recover "the consideration paid for the security

. . . upon the tender back of the security" or could sue for damages if they no longer owned the security. The Securities Act was bitterly opposed by the financial interests and repeated efforts were made to compel its repeal on the ground that it prevented the orderly movement of capital into new industrial enterprises. This contention probably had some merit; but the chief reason for the failure of savings to seek new investment outlets, during the period of the New Deal, was simply excess plant capacity. The act was amended in the Securities Exchange Act of 1934 to weaken very considerably the liability of underwriters, officers, and directors because of misleading and false statements; also, persons suing to recover damages might be required to post bonds.

Another outstanding reform was the enactment of a measure, signed June 6, 1934, for the regulation of the stock exchanges of the country. The act, as J. F. Dewhurst and M. G. Schneider in the *Nation* of March 14, 1934, pointed out, had three major objectives: (1) "to limit the volume of speculation by restricting the amount of credit available for trading in securities; (2) to prevent dishonest and improper dealing by eliminating manipulation and by limiting the trading activities of persons in privileged positions on the exchanges and of officers of corporations whose securities are traded in; (3) to protect the interests of the investor by requiring more adequate information on corporations and their securities and thereby raising the standards of corporate management and accounting practice."

The Securities Exchange Act, among other things, provided for: the establishment of a Securities and Exchange Commission to be appointed by the President by and with the consent of the Senate; the licensing of stock exchanges by the commission; the vesting of the Federal Reserve Board with power to prescribe rules "with respect to the amount of credit that may be initially extended and subsequently maintained on any security"; for the initial extension of credit, that is, for marginal loans, the standard was to be as follows: at an amount not greater than, whichever is the higher of—(1) 55 per cent of current market prices, or (2) 100 per cent of the security's lowest market price in three years (but not more than 75 per cent of the current market price); restrictions on borrowing by members of national securities exchanges, brokers, and dealers; prohibitions against the manipulation of prices; liability at law to customers by dealers or brokers giving false statements about securities; the formulation by the commission of rules regulating short sales and stop-loss orders; similar rules regulating or preventing members from floor trading for their own account; and in other ways segregating and limiting the functions of members, brokers, and dealers. All listed securities were to be registered with the commission and information was to be furnished about the organization, financial structure, and nature of the business performed; the kinds of securities outstanding; the size of the interest of directors, officers, and underwriters in the securities; bonus and profit-sharing arrangements; management and service contracts; balance sheets; profit and loss statements, and the like.

MISCELLANEOUS AGENCIES

The railroad legislation of the country also received the attention of the New Deal. The Emergency Railroad Transportation Act, which was approved June 16, 1933, contained many marked departures from customary governmental railroad policy. These were at once apparent in the stated purposes of the act, which were as follows:

(1) To encourage and promote or require action on the part of the carriers and of subsidiaries subject to the Interstate Commerce Act, as amended, which will (a) avoid unnecessary duplication of services and facilities of whatsoever nature and permit the joint use of terminals and trackage incident thereto or requisite to such joint use: Provided, that no routes now existing shall be eliminated except with the consent of all participating lines or upon order of the Coördinator, (b) control allowances, accessorial services and the charges therefor, and other practices affecting service or operation, to the end that undue impairment of net earnings may be prevented, and (c) avoid other wastes and preventable expense;

(2) To promote financial reorganization of the carriers, with due regard to legal rights, so as to reduce fixed charges to the extent required by the public interest and improve carrier credit; and

(3) To provide for the immediate study of other means of improving conditions surrounding transportation in all its forms and the preparation of plans therefor.

The new law made provision for the establishment of a Federal Coördinator of Transportation, placed railroad holding companies under the supervision of the Interstate Commerce Commission, and repealed the famous recapture clause of the Transportation Act of 1920. To advise with the Coördinator there were set up regional coördinating committees for the East, West, and South; each such committee was to be made up of five regular and two special members, the latter representing the short lines and the electric lines. Certain labor protective clauses were inserted in the law placing restrictions on reductions in the number of employees in the service of a carrier and in their compensation. Joseph B. Eastman, who was appointed Coördinator, in a report to Congress indicated it as his belief that government ownership and operation was likely to be the only solution of the railroad problem; however, he was not prepared to make such a recommendation for the time being because the financial strain of possessing the railroads would probably be too great.

One of the New Deal's most interesting experiments in social planning was the creation of the Tennessee Valley Authority on May 18, 1933. This agency, which grew out of the administration's decision to utilize to the full the potentialities of the Muscle Shoals development, was given the right to generate and sell power (largely for the purpose of acting as a yardstick against which the rates of private utilities could be measured); build dams, power plants, and transmission lines; develop fertilizers; and also lay out a general program for promoting the social and economic welfare of the seven states in the Tennessee Valley region (Tennessee, Virginia, North Carolina, Georgia, Alabama, Mississippi, and Kentucky). Among other activities in this general scheme of rehabilitation were to be the prevention of soil erosion, reforestation, the balancing of agriculture and industry, the better and fuller use of mineral resources, the vocational education of populations, and the establishment of subsistence homesteads. The TVA was given originally a grant of $50,000,000 from the funds of the PWA and the first comprehensive plan on which it began work was the supplying of cheap electrical power to the residents of the states in the region who were within transmission distance of the plant already at Muscle Shoals in Alabama and the one being erected at the Norris Dam in Tennessee. The government also created a corporation known as the Electric Home and Farm Authority, as a subsidiary of the TVA, for the purpose of stimulating the use of electrical appliances and the consumption of electrical power;

among other functions, the corporation was to assist in financing the purchase by consumers of efficient electrical equipment at very low prices. Another agency working with the TVA was the Tennessee Valley Associated Coöperatives, which was to aid coöperative groups in the region. In July, 1934, as an example of the sort of programs it was going to foster, the TVA bought out the electric power properties of the Tennessee Public Service Co., which was serving Knoxville, Tenn. and its immediate vicinity; the intention was to sell these plants to the city of Knoxville and to the other communities directly served.

The Home Owners' Refinancing Act, approved June 13, 1933, and the Home Owners' Loan Act, approved April 27, 1934, set up two agencies to extend relief to home owners either in danger of losing their homes through foreclosure of mortgages or incapable of making necessary improvements because of their inability to obtain financing. The first of these agencies, the Home Owners' Loan Corporation, was to serve the needs of home owners; the second, the Federal Savings and Loan Associations, was to provide funds for home construction. The Home Owners' Loan Corporation refinanced mortgage debts in those cases where the principal of the mortgage had become due or where the mortgage had been foreclosed within a period of two years of the date of application. It did this by offering to exchange its bonds, guaranteed by the government as to principal and interest, for the instrument of the mortgagee; the mortgagee, however, had to accept bonds not exceeding 80 per cent of the value of the property as appraised by the corporation's agents. The maximum was to be $14,000. The previous mortgages and all other liens were then converted into a single first mortgage secured by the home and held by the corporation. Interest was to be at 5 per cent and principal was to be repaid in fifteen years, the corporation having the right to grant an extension of principal or interest to a home owner where there was justification. In addition, the corporation could make cash loans, not to exceed 40 per cent of the value of properties, to retire an existing mortgage when there was danger of foreclosure; and also advance on unencumbered properties cash for taxes, maintenance, and repairs not in excess of 50 per cent of the appraised values. Limited loans might be made for the purpose of recovering homes for original owners who had lost them by foreclosure or forced sale subsequent to January 1, 1930. The corporation's capital stock of $200,000,000 was entirely subscribed by the Treasury and it was permitted to issue bonds up to $2,000,000,000 to exchange for mortgages.

Starting off slowly, chiefly because an appraisal machinery had to be built up and because mortgagees were loath to accept the corporation's bonds which originally were guaranteed only as to interest, by the end of 1933 the corporation was functioning with commendable speed. At the end of June, 1934, it had succeeded in refinancing 340,000 home mortgages and had made advances totaling $1,028,000,000; 99 per cent of the transactions had been effected by the exchange of the guaranteed bonds of the HOLC for past due mortgages. The average loan made was $3,013. The total number of applications had been more than 1,500,000 and requests for refinancing had involved $4,856,000,000. The Federal Savings and Loan Associations were local, mutual thrift, and financing agencies sponsored by the government; funds were obtained from the sale of shares and shareholders borrowed money using their shares as security.

Of even greater significance, as far as relief of home owners was concerned, was the passage of the National Housing bill on June 18, 1934 (approved June 28). This provided a thoroughgoing scheme of home financing and mortgage insurance and offered protection to financial institutions making loans for financing alterations, repairs, and improvements. A program of mutual mortgage insurance (covering first mortgages on residential property which were being amortized) was set up; and there were authorized national mortgage associations with the right to purchase and sell first mortgages and borrow money through the issue of securities up to ten times their outstanding capital value or the current face value of the mortgages they held. Further, there was created a corporation for the purpose of insuring accounts of building and loan associations. The government was authorized to guarantee up to 20 per cent of $1,000,000,000 of private loans for home repairs; while the $2,000,000,000 borrowing power of the HOLC was increased by $1,000,000,000, of which $300,000,000 was to be for loans for repairs. A Federal Housing Administrator was to be appointed by the President to administer the housing renovation and modernization, the mutual mortgage insurance, and the national mortgage association features of the act.

To cope with the many relief problems arising out of the general unemployment, the collapse of private philanthropy, and the inability of local jurisdictions to provide cash and work aid to families, single persons, and transients, Congress set up the Federal Emergency Relief Administration on May 12, 1933. An initial appropriation of $500,000,000 was voted and a second one for $950,000,000 was approved by the President on February 15, 1934. Half of the first appropriation was to be spent on a matching basis, that is, one federal dollar for every three from all public sources within the state itself; the other half was to be used for grants to states whose relief needs were so great as to make necessary some funds in addition to the matched allotments; in almost all cases, the funds were to be administered and grants to families made by the local public relief agencies. The FERA provided for some three hundred relief centers for transients; these shelters were under the general supervision of state relief administrations, although in many cases they were conducted by the transients themselves. Grants in aid were made also to self-help groups of unemployed.

In November, 1933, in order to provide work at regular salaries for 4,000,000 unemployed men and women, at least half of whom were already on relief rolls, the Civil Works Administration was established. This agency was financed in part from $400,-000,000 allocated from the funds of the PWA, and its original plan was to put persons to work on public works projects. Because of the speed with which the whole scheme was devised, however, many of the projects were of a made-work character. The hours of labor and wage rates were originally fixed by the FERA; in February, 1934, Congress provided that the rate of pay was to be at a minimum of 30 cents an hour and that the hours of labor were to be not more than 24 a week in urban areas and 15 in rural areas. Beginning in February the CWA was demobilized, the process being completed by March 31, 1934. The ostensible reason cited by Washington was the readiness of private industry to absorb the CWA workers. The real reasons, probably, were an unwillingness to build up a federal system of made-work relief which might be made permanent and the fear that the CWA workers could easily be organized to agitate for better pay and working conditions, if not for really radical purposes. Persons on CWA projects were then transferred back to the work divisions of local relief administrations.

Another relief device was the creation of the Federal Surplus Relief Corporation, in October, 1933, for the purpose of (1) relieving the emergency through the purchase, processing, and distribution for consumption of agricultural and other commodities, and (2) utilizing surpluses of foodstuffs, clothing, fuel, etc. in the relief of the unemployed. Surplus agricultural products were received from the AAA and were paid for from the processing taxes; other commodities were purchased with relief funds to provide essentials for the needy. Up to the end of 1933 the following were the outstanding commodities distributed to the states for allocation among unemployed families: 89,927,000 pounds of salt pork; 8,647,000 pounds of smoked pork; 38,444,000 pounds of flour; 5,992,000 pounds of butter; 4,130,000 pounds of beans.

On June 8, 1934, shortly before the Seventy-third Congress' regular session adjourned after five and one-half months of continuous labor, President Roosevelt indicated that certain pieces of social legislation would yet have to be passed before the New Deal's work in recovery and reform could be regarded as having been completed; but these would have to wait for the next Congress' convening in January, 1935. Basic to any program of social reconstruction—"a minimum of the promise that we can offer to the American people," said the President—was the "security of the men, women, and children of the nation"; and this was to be attained by three means: adequate housing, relocation of populations so that opportunities for productive work were afforded to all, and protection against unemployment and old age. As regards the first, Congress already had before it a measure to stimulate the private lending of money for the modernization of existing homes and the building of new ones (the National Housing Act, described above). With respect to the second, what was imperative was a full utilization of all our knowledge of the country's soil and weather conditions and a transplanting of peoples from areas where the struggles for a livelihood were confronted by insuperable obstacles to other areas where at least a living could be earned. "When the next Congress convenes," promised the President, "I hope to be able to present to it a carefully considered national plan, covering the development and the human use of our national resources of land and water over a longer period of years."

As regards the third, a program of social insurance was imperative. The President was not definite as to the methods to be employed in setting up and operating the machinery but he laid down the following general principles: there ought to be a "maximum of coöperation between the state and federal governments"; the funds "should be raised by contribution rather than by an increase in general taxation" (this in spite of the fact that all the existing state old age pension systems in the country were entirely based on taxation); social insurance was to be national in scope, "although the several states should meet at least a large portion of the cost of management, leaving to the federal government the responsibility of investing, maintaining, and safeguarding the funds constituting the necessary insurance reserves."

All this did not constitute a change in values: the United States was not going socialist. And the President took pains to assure the country that the government would gladly relinquish many of its burdens if "private investment and private initiative" would only step forward to assume them. He went on to say: "We have not imposed undue restrictions upon business. We have not opposed the incentive of reasonable and legitimate private profit." There can be no question that President Roosevelt meant all this sincerely: that he sought to guarantee Americans the rights to their homes, livelihoods, and individual security; and that, equally, he was devoted to the maintenance of the capitalist system.

The New Deal, Foreign Trade, and Foreign Policy

The triumph, at the World Economic Conference, of nationalism over internationalism did not mean that defenders of the latter policy had accepted their setback as a final and irrevocable one. They persevered—and this was particularly true of Secretaries Hull and Wallace—so that gradually the President began to yield from the extreme position he had taken at the time of the London Conference in July. By December, Secretary Hull had won back so much lost ground that when he appeared at Montevideo, Uruguay, at the head of the American delegation to the seventh Pan-American Conference, he could openly express the United States' interest once more in the expansion of foreign trade and credits.

In proposing that all nations join in eliminating useless trade barriers and reducing tariffs, the Secretary boldly declared that his suggestion was "based upon the conviction that full, stable, and durable business recovery can only be effected by the restoration of international trade and finance to an extent mutually profitable." The Secretary had two methods to offer toward this end: the adoption of bilateral, or reciprocal, treaties and the simultaneous destruction of obstacles to trade by all the important commercial nations. To hasten the latter, in particular, he continued to be a staunch defender of the most-favored-nation clause in its unconditional form, or the principle of equality of treatment.

To Secretary Hull's support, as has been said, came Secretary Wallace: and in February, 1934, he voiced an eloquent plea for the reëstablishment of foreign intercourse in his pamphlet "America Must Choose." Not on the old basis, naturally, of the free flow of goods, services, and capital investments: Adam Smith and Richard Cobden had proved to be false prophets. But what the new United States must strive for was a "planned middle course," or "a neighborhood of trade," which, operating through reciprocal trading arrangements,—"with actual goods exchanged, not goods for promises to be collected later on at any cost"—would permit us to lower our tariff walls for the admission of some $500,000,000 more in imports than reached us in 1929 and in return would find customers for our agricultural wares. An early example of what the Department of State had in mind was the signing of a bilateral trade convention with Colombia. In this agreement, the United States promised an open market for Colombia's chief export, coffee, by keeping it on the free list; Colombia, on its part, promised to purchase in the United States a corresponding amount of products which it normally imported. Negotiations leading to similar understandings were under way with Cuba, Brazil, Argentina, Sweden, and Portugal.

With the opening of the new year the President made further concessions to the international element. Two new policies in an expansionist program were announced: the United States was going to make a bid for foreign markets by the setting up of public banking corporations to finance foreign trade and by executive control of tariff policy. Two such banks, the so-called Export-Import Bank of Washington, D. C. and the Second Export-Import Bank of Washington, D. C., the first to extend credit facilities to all business men desiring to sell to Russia and the second to do similarly in the case of Cuba, were established in February and March respectively; it was subsequently announced that the second bank would also finance trade with all other countries. George N. Peek, who was made president of the institutions, promised to push vigorously the sale of American farm and industrial surpluses abroad; his statement announcing the opening of the first bank declared in part: [2]

Due to changing conditions throughout the world, government can and should assist in many directions in the conduct of a sound international trade. I urge industry in its own interest to be temperate in its demands and I invite its fullest coöperation. I want to make it clear that this bank has been created for the purpose of assisting our foreign trade and of providing facilities, not now obtainable in regular banking channels, for financing the seller. . . . Eventually, exports and imports must balance.

As regards the executive control of tariff policy, President Roosevelt asked Congress for the power to adjust existing tariff rates —not lower than or in excess of 50 per cent of the present duties— for the purpose of permitting bargaining with foreign nations toward the effecting of bilateral trade agreements. This right was granted in June, 1934. It was significant to note that a number of Republican leaders, notably former Secretary of the Treasury O. L. Mills and former Secretary of State H. L. Stimson, came to the support of the President; thus there were indications that the Republican party might be led to champion the internationalist cause after having steadfastly defended the isolationist position, as regards tariff protection, for more than seventy years. If this reversal was to occur it could be said that the predominant economic interest of the country was no longer industry but finance, no longer

[2] The Export-Import Bank never got started in its business of financing Russian trade as a result of the decision of its administrators that they would abide by the Johnson Debt Default Act (approved April 13, 1934), which forbade the sale in this country of securities issued by governments which were in default in the payment of their obligations to the United States. This was, of course, only technically true of Russia, for the Russian debt had been contracted not by the Soviets but by the Kerensky government. The move was interpreted as a device for compelling Russia to come to an agreement with the United States over the governmental debts and private claims outstanding. Americans were estimating that the debt and claims totaled $600,000,000.

industrial capitalism but finance capitalism. Mr. Mills' speech, on January 29, 1934, was frankness itself. In it, he said:

I prefer to turn my attention to the possibilities, among others, of recovering lost markets and to the stimulation of increased consumption not only through the restoration of purchasing power at home but through the promotion of a greater prosperity and a higher standard of living the world over. Granted that the difficulties are enormous and that much time and patience will be required, this is even more true of the self-containment program. We will have to abandon the present policy of isolation and intense nationalism and to some extent modify recent tariff practices.

The boldness of the New Deal's domestic policies had its counterpart in the field of foreign affairs, although, here too, achievement was not on the credit side of the ledger entirely. Russia was recognized; the Philippines received their independence; the date for American withdrawal from Haiti was definitely fixed; the Platt Amendment, as regards Cuba, was repealed; and a pledge was given to our Latin-American neighbors that the United States would never again resort to armed intervention in the territories of the other republics of the Western Hemisphere. On the other hand, relations with Japan continued to be strained; the Administration launched a big-navy program which was bound to have unfortunate repercussions abroad; and the President insisted upon playing politics with the intergovernmental war debts, refusing to recognize publicly what every one already knew—that the debts had in effect already been defaulted and would never be paid.

The reëstablishment of diplomatic relations with Russia constituted the Administration's greatest triumph in its intercourse with foreign countries and ended the policy of non-recognition that had endured since the downfall of the Kerensky government in 1917. President Roosevelt himself took the initiative and at his request Commissar for Foreign Affairs Litvinoff journeyed to Washington to explore with the President all questions outstanding between the two countries. Conversations began on November 7, 1933 and continued until November 17, when diplomatic relations were formally reopened with an exchange of notes.

The notes committed both governments to respect the territorial integrity of each other and not to tolerate within their borders

organizations which had as their aim "the overthrow of, or bringing about by force of a change in the political or social order" of
the other. Russia also guaranteed the right of Americans to wor-
ship in their own churches; and each country agreed that in the
event of the arrest of their respective nationals in the other's country the consuls would be notified at once by the authorities. Russia
waived all claims for American military activities in the Siberian
intervention after the World War, while other financial claims and
counter-claims were to be negotiated between the new Russian ambassador to Washington and the State Department. William C.
Bullitt, who had been attached to the American Peace Commission at Versailles in 1919 and who had broken with Wilson over the
peace treaty, was named the first American ambassador to Soviet
Russia; A. A. Troyanovsky, who was vice-chairman of the Russian State Planning Commission and prior to that had been ambassador to Japan, was named the Russian envoy to the United
States.

A bill for Philippine independence, the so-called Hawes-Cutting
bill, after years of agitation, had finally been passed by Congress
on December 29, 1932, had been vetoed by President Hoover
on January 13, 1933, and four days later had become law by re-
passage over the Presidential veto. The measure provided for the
establishment of a transitional commonwealth, in effect as an
American protectorate, for a period of approximately twelve years
and under a Filipino chief executive. The United States retained
the right to maintain military posts and naval bases in the islands
and decisions by the insular courts were to be subject to review by
the United States Supreme Court. During the probationary period
the free entry of most Philippine imports into the United States
was to cease and regular tariff rates were to be imposed on Philippine sugar, cocoanut oil, and fibers in excess of certain fixed quotas;
on all duty-free articles exported to the United States an excise tax
was to be put for the purpose of servicing the Philippine public
debts; also Philippine immigrants virtually were to be barred from
the United States.

The Hawes-Cutting Act called upon the Philippine legislature
to accept the independence measure within one year; in October,
1933, both houses of the island assembly voted it down. Senator
Quezon, in the Philippine senate, expressed the general opposition

of the islanders when he characterized the law as follows: "It is not an independence bill at all; it is a tariff directed against our products; it is an immigration bill directed against our labor." On March 2, 1934, President Roosevelt reopened the question when he urged upon Congress to revive the Hawes-Cutting bill. Amendments, however, were to be included to provide for the removal of the American military reservations from the islands and to leave the question of the continuance of our naval bases to future negotiations with a Philippine government. Roosevelt said nothing of the economic and immigration sections of the old law, thus brushing aside the chief complaints of Filipinos against the independence measure. The Tydings-McDuffie bill, introduced in Congress and signed by the President on March 24, was substantially the Hawes-Cutting law except that the military and naval sections were changed in harmony with the President's recommendations. On May 1, 1934, the Philippine legislature, bowing to the inevitable and regarding independence as a mixed blessing, gave its approval. A few days later Filipinos were to see what independence really meant: for Congress, in passing the Revenue Act of 1934, included a prohibitive excise tax on Philippine cocoanut oil and copra, thus crippling an industry on which perhaps 3,000,000 out of the total Philippine population of 14,000,000 depended.

In the field of Latin-American affairs the President proceeded to carry out the "good neighbor" pledge which he had made in his inaugural address. Indeed, at a Woodrow Wilson memorial dinner on December 28, 1933, Roosevelt went so far as to promise openly, thus definitely consigning the (Theodore) Roosevelt Corollary of the Monroe Doctrine to the limbo of forgotten diplomatic things, the following:

. . . the definite policy of the United States from now on is one opposed to armed intervention. The maintenance of constitutional government in other nations is not a sacred obligation devolving upon the United States alone. The maintenance of law and the orderly processes of government in this hemisphere is the concern of each individual nation within its own borders first of all. It is only if and when the failure of orderly processes of government affects the other nations of the continent that it becomes their concern; and the point to stress is that in such event it becomes the joint concern of a whole continent in which we are all neighbors.

In line with the above, Washington promised to withdraw the last of the American marines from Haiti before the end of 1934; and on May 31, 1934, the Senate ratified a treaty with Cuba under which the Platt Amendment was abrogated. This had followed a decidedly obscure interlude in Cuban-American relations. The Cuban dictator Machado had been driven into exile in August, 1933, as a result of a general uprising; and, thanks to the support given him by the American Ambassador Sumner Welles, the conservative De Cespedes had been elevated to the presidency over the wishes of most of the Cuban population. Another revolt soon took place, De Cespedes hurriedly resigned, and a liberal government, supported by the army and the students and headed by Ramón Grau San Martin, was installed. While the United States carefully refrained from intervention and American destroyers policing Cuban waters did not land marines, intervention in effect took place, for the refusal of the American State Department to recognize Grau—presumably on the ground that he could not be expected to maintain the peace and carry out Cuba's international obligations—brought about his downfall four months after he had come into office. When Grau was succeeded by Carlos Mendieta, who in many respects soon demonstrated that he was no better than Machado, recognition by Washington followed in four days; it was hard therefore to down the suspicion that Grau had been unfavorably regarded because he would not yield to American pressure while Mendieta was supported because he would, and that the Platt Amendment had been suddenly repealed to strengthen Mendieta's slipping hold on Cuban affairs. From the American point of view, the handling of the affair was hardly creditable.

While American dealings with Japan outwardly remained friendly and the two governments through their foreign offices and official spokesmen from time to time exchanged formal sentiments of mutual regard, there were ample evidences to indicate that distrustfulness of each other reigned at Washington and Tokyo. American refusal to recognize the Japanese puppet state Manchoukuo, our new friendliness toward Russia, and our continued interest in China's welfare were at the basis of Japanese hostility; Americans, on their part, appeared to be concerned about Japanese naval ambitions and the apparent intention of Japan, sooner or later, to overawe the whole of China. Put in realistic rather than diplomatic language, the quarrel, as yet not officially stated, was based on the rivalry of two great imperialist powers for domination in the Far East.

On April 17, 1934, Japan unmasked its ambitions when the spokesman of the Japanese foreign office issued a statement that his country could not permit China to receive financial, military, and technical assistance from foreign individuals or foreign governments whose purpose was to help China resist Japan. The declaration specifically made mention of aid for war purposes and the lending of money "to provide funds for political uses"; and it disclaimed any thought of Japanese interference with "any foreign country's negotiating individually with China on questions of finance or trade as long as such negotiations benefit China and are not detrimental to peace in Eastern Asia." But the threat behind the statement was obvious and it was so understood in the United States. As the *American Observer* phrased it: "Reduced to its simplest terms this blunt declaration meant that Japan considers China her own back yard and other nations must be careful how they play in it."

The Japanese foreign office manifesto met with immediate rejoinders from abroad. Great Britain and France asked for official confirmations, while the United States sent a polite but firm memorandum in which our State Department pointed to the fact that the territorial integrity of China was guaranteed by international law, the Nine-Power Treaty of 1922 (which also underwrote the Open Door policy), and the Kellogg-Briand pact for the outlawing of war. Japanese Foreign Minister Koki Hirota, in his reply, was more circumspect in outlining the Japanese position —but he did not yield an inch. Japan adhered to the Nine-Power Treaty, respected the Open Door, and had no designs on Chinese territory; nor did Japan have any intentions of interfering with the trade between China and the Occident where that trade was to China's benefit. However, it was Japan's duty to maintain peace in China; and Japan would frown on the attempts by other powers to "exploit" China and would resent any trade or movements which would permit the Chinese to disturb the peace of Eastern Asia. On this uncertain note the interchange of diplomatic communications ended, with the two powers continuing to watch each other suspiciously across the Pacific. This was particularly true of their naval programs.

The intention of Japan, in 1935, to denounce the Washington and London Naval Limitation Treaties and to ask for parity, at least as far as naval strength in the Western Pacific was concerned, was already known; on the other hand, the Roosevelt Administration embarked upon a costly naval building program, the largest one in the peace-time history of the country. On the ground that every ton was justified by the two naval treaties, the Administration asked and Congress readily granted appropriations involving the expenditure of close to $1,000,000,000 over five years (by the Vinson Naval Parity Act, approved March 27, 1934). At the beginning of 1934, 32 destroyers, 11 cruisers, 6 submarines, 3 aircraft carriers, and 2 gunboats were already under construction, while 102 additional warships had been authorized. The President was also to "procure the necessary aircraft for vessels and other purposes in numbers commensurate with a treaty navy." Defenders of the Administration's course denied that the building program was really preparing the way for a naval race with Japan and Great Britain; they insisted that the United States could be in a position to bargain for real limitation in 1935 only if it had a navy second to none. In many quarters the argument was frankly regarded as spurious but so real had a war scare become that there was no concerted effort to defeat the navy bill in Congress.

The intergovernmental war debt controversy continued to trouble international waters. In the six months of July to December, 1932, which followed the end of the Hoover moratorium, requests for the postponement of payments came from Great Britain, France, Belgium, Czechoslovakia, Estonia, Latvia, Lithuania, and Poland. These President Hoover declined to honor with the result that Belgium, Estonia, France, and Poland refused to make the regular payments on December 15, 1932. Czechoslovakia, Finland, Great Britain, Italy, Latvia, and Lithuania met their payments, Great Britain, however, pointing out that this would be the last such until a new settlement was effected. On June 15, 1933, all the nations, except Finland, Great Britain and Italy, defaulted. Finland paid its full installment, while Great Britain and Italy made only token payments, the former of $10,000,000 and the latter of $1,000,000; at this time President Roosevelt assured Great Britain and Italy that he would not regard them as being in technical default. The same procedure took place on December

15, 1933. But between that date and June 15, 1933, Congress had passed the Johnson Debt Default Act which refused to regard token payments as an adequate fulfillment of the obligations of the debtor nations; the President's hands were tied unless Congress consented to release him.

Roosevelt's message of June 1, 1934, however, refused to ask for new legislation: the President was thus taking the position that the debts were to be repaid. He said: "These obligations furnished vital means for the successful conclusion of a war which involved the national existence of the borrowers, and later for a quicker restoration of their normal life after the war ended." The money, in turn, had been borrowed from the American people. "It is for these reasons that the American people have felt that their debtors were called upon to make a determined effort to discharge these obligations." And the American people, the President hinted broadly, could not be lenient as long as the European nations continued to spend such vast sums on the building up of their military and naval establishments. When Great Britain, in reply, announced the complete suspension of payments pending a final revision of the settlement, the vexing question of the war debts was once more clamoring for attention.

The Cost of the New Deal

In a budget statement submitted to Congress on January 4, 1934, President Roosevelt indicated that the difficulty of an unbalanced budget was not going to stand in the way of the realization of the New Deal program. His plans for the fiscal years 1933–34 and 1934–35 called for the balancing of the ordinary budget, made up of the usual civil and military expenditures, and resort to borrowing to carry the items on the extraordinary budget. These estimates assumed that, for 1933–34, the ordinary receipts would be $3,260,000,000, the ordinary expenditures $3,046,000,000, and the extraordinary expenditures $7,523,000,000. The deficit for the year would thus be $7,309,000,000. For the year 1934–35, with the industrial situation of the country presumably improved and revenues therefore higher, the ordinary receipts would be $4,455,-000,000, the ordinary expenditures $3,237,000,000, and the extraordinary expenditures $3,204,000,000. The deficit would then be $1,986,000,000,000. For the fiscal year following the President expected that the budget could be balanced. The cost of the New Deal would thus raise the country's gross debt from the $22,539,-000,000 on July 1, 1933, to $31,834,000,000 on July 1, 1935.

But, at the end of the fiscal year 1933–34, the position of the Treasury revealed an astonishing state of affairs. Instead of having expended $7,500,000,000 for extraordinary purposes and to speed recovery, the government had not spent much more than $4,000,-000,000. Thus, the public gross debt stood only at $27,053,000,000 on June 30, 1934; while this was the highest point ever reached by the national debt it was considerably below the President's estimate. The PWA program had moved more slowly than had been anticipated; the RFC had made fewer loans to private borrowers; relief expenditures were scarcely adequate in view of the great amount of distress still existing in the country.[3] The government apparently was curtailing its emergency spending despite the fact that the farmer's dollar was nowhere near parity and there still existed more than 11,000,000 industrial unemployed. The sharp criticism which at once was provoked led to the President's asking the House Appropriations Committee to give him complete control over the RFC's savings and unobligated balances; the sum thus available might have been as great as $4,000,000,000. But the Senate, in amending the Deficiency Appropriation bill, in June, 1934, saw fit to allow Roosevelt the use of but $500,000,000 of the RFC fund for relief purposes. The result was the President had approximately $3,716,000,000 to expend for emergency and rehabilitation programs during 1934–35; this amount was not very much more than his estimate of January 4, 1934.

The taxation program of the Administration, on the other hand, did not impose oppressive burdens on the wealthy. The Revenue Act of 1934, approved May 10, 1934, estimated an increase of, at the most, $417,000,000 during a full year's operation from increased taxes on capital. The new law substituted a flat normal rate of 4 per cent on all net income on the first $4,000 and 8 per cent on the remainder, and started the surtax at 4 per cent on net income above $4,000 instead of 1 per cent on incomes in excess of $6,000. It placed a maximum surtax of 59 per cent on incomes in excess of $1,000,000, as in the existing law, but rearranged the

---

[3] The chief emergency expenditures during 1933–34 had been as follows: RFC, $1,615,000,000; PWA, $640,000,000; CWA, $720,000,000; CCC, $320,000,000; FERA, $360,000,000; miscellaneous, $380,000,000.

brackets so as to give a slight decrease to the average taxpayer whose income was less than $30,000. Estate tax rates were to run from 1 to 60 per cent instead of the prevailing 1 to 45 per cent. A different treatment of capital gains and losses was provided so as to yield an additional $30,000,000 in a full year; a special tax of 30 and 40 per cent was imposed on the adjusted net income of personal holding companies; and consolidated returns for all corporations except railroads were eliminated.

IV. THE NEW DEAL IN PRACTICE: IN AGRICULTURE

The Course of Recovery

From the middle of March, 1933, up to the end of July, 1933, the heavens seemed to smile on the New Deal. A definite upturn evidenced itself in better agricultural prices, resumption of industrial activity, and the reëmployment of labor. What if a number of doubting voices were raised to the effect that among the factors of recovery the Administration program was of minor influence: that the change for the better in American economic conditions merely reflected a general world-wide improvement; that the feeling that inflation was impending gave a buoyancy to prices of commodities and securities and encouraged freer spending; that industrialists and distributors, anticipating higher raw material and labor costs as a result of the operation of the processing taxes and codes, rushed to resume fabrication on the one hand and to replenish stocks on the other? Recovery, whatever the reasons, was on the way.

From March to July, industrial production increased 66 per cent, factory employment increased 23 per cent, factory payrolls increased 35 per cent. Of course there were certain disquieting elements in the situation, clouds no bigger than a man's hand, but it was generally felt that in time these would be dispelled. The gain in industrial production from March to July was three times as rapid as the gain in factory employment and almost twice as rapid as the gain in factory payrolls. Also, industrial production, as compared with the 1923–25 average, had almost reached normal, while the employment index stood at only 69 and the index for factory payrolls was still as low as 50. It was further true that the industrial improvement was largely taking place in the consumers' goods industries—food, leather, paper, textiles, tobacco, and the like—where even the depression itself had brought about no serious curtailments in activity. The capital goods industries—steel, machinery, metals, lumber, cement, and the like—on the other hand, re-

mained stagnant or gained but little despite the public works program, loans to railroads for equipment, the resumption of naval
building, and the utilization of a large sum of money for army
housing. Nothing revealed the situation more plainly than the inability of long-term credits to find new sources of investment. In
1929, more than $10,000,000,000 in new stock and bond issues had
been floated, of which $9,400,000,000 had been for domestic pur-
poses. By 1932 such long-term financing operations had dropped
to $1,165,000,000, with most of the total being in domestic issues.
During the first seven months of 1933, the flow of new credit
reached a total of only $401,000,000. But there was a real ray of
hope coming from the agricultural regions. In February, prices
received by farmers were 49 per cent of the prewar level and prices
paid were 100 per cent, making the farm index of purchasing power
49 per cent of that prevailing during 1909–14. By July, however,
prices received had mounted to 76 per cent, and prices paid only
to 103 per cent, with the result that the index of purchasing power
had bounded up to 72 per cent of the assumed normal.

The Administration, thus heartened, rapidly pushed its program
of cartelization in industry through the code-making procedure
and raised no serious objection to the growing frequency of strikes
on the part of organized labor. The institutional advance, at any
rate, was taking place on all fronts; the feeling that the class balance could be maintained was reflected constantly in the sanguine
statements and inspired reports coming out of Washington.

With August, however, the gains began slowly to fritter away;
by the end of the year, very little remained. Industrial production
in December stood at 75 per cent (adjusted) of the 1923–25 average, as compared with 92 per cent in June and 100 per cent in
July; the factory employment index had scarcely moved, being
74 in December as compared with 67 in June and 72 in July; factory payrolls were 55 per cent of normal in December as compared with 47 in June and 51 in July; the entrance of new money
into capital enterprises in December totaled only $57,000,000.
Prices continued to climb, however, with the result that September was the first month to show a decrease in real wages. The retail trades also failed to improve because of the resistance of consumers to higher prices.

By December, from labor's point of view, it seemed that the
gains were not much more than illusory. True, an estimated 3,000,-

ooo wage earners had been put back to work out of a total of possibly 15,000,000 unemployed persons at the lowest point in the depression in March, 1933. But great numbers of these, it was generally being charged, had been reëmployed at the low minimums fixed in the codes so that the prescribed minimums had become the maximums only too frequently.[1] The American Federation of Labor, surveying the situation on November 4, reported that from March to the end of September a 6 per cent increase in total wages had occurred; but, it was forced to admit, this had been more than swallowed up by an increase of 8.5 per cent in the cost of living. Recovery by restoration of purchasing power through a just price for labor had not been achieved. The fixing of minimum wages and maximum hours in the codes, in the eyes of many, had turned out to be another share-the-work scheme on a national basis.

The farm situation was decidedly worse. Farm prices began to fall sharply, wheat dropping at Chicago in one week in October, for example, from 85 cents a bushel to 69 cents and cotton at New York from 9.42 cents a pound to 8.58 cents. At the end of the year farm prices were 32 per cent under the prewar average while the prices the farmer paid were 16 per cent above, making the farm index of purchasing power 59 per cent of the assumed normal as compared with 53 per cent a whole year before. Despite all the hopeful talk of the establishment of parity prices for agriculture as the way out of the depression, in the middle of October, after elaborate programs in some instances had been working more than half a year, the following were the proportions of parity which producers of leading farm commodities were receiving: wheat, current farm prices 66 per cent of parity; cotton, 61.8 per cent of parity; corn, 48.1 per cent of parity; butter fat, 68.6 per cent of parity; beef cattle, 60.1 per cent of parity; hogs, 51.7 per cent of parity.

With the beginning of 1934, another upturn began, but on a decidedly lower level than that of the period of March–July, 1933. In March, 1934, the adjusted index of industrial production stood at 85 as compared with 84 in September, 1933; true, it

[1] On this point it is illuminating to note an observation made by the Labor Advisory Board in May, 1934: ". . . employed workers receiving more than the minimum have not shared in the recovery as much as was expected. 'Equitable Adjustment' clauses [in the codes] have not been effectual and action should be taken to promote this necessary means of increasing labor income."

was 42 per cent above the bottom of the depression but 33 per cent below the peak of 1929. The *New Republic,* in commenting on this state of affairs, pointed out:

In ordinary depressions, production does not drop so much as 33 per cent from peak to trough. And we must remember two important facts regarding the peak 1929 production: (1) since the population has increased in the past five years, a higher production than in 1929 would be necessary to supply the same amount of goods per capita, and (2) since advances in efficiency have greatly increased output per man-hour, a much larger production than in 1929 would be necessary to furnish the same number of man-hours of employment. (The advance in output per man-hour in these years was approximately 25 per cent. Though some of this advance may be lost as employment grows, by no means all of it will be.)

Other indexes were not very much more hopeful. The index of construction contracts awarded, which rose from 14 in March, 1933 to 57 in December, 1933, fell back to 33 in March, 1934. Factory employment and payrolls were a little better, the former rising to 81 of the 1923–25 normal and the latter to 65, by March, 1934. But the individual worker in industry made no real gains, measured by the standard of real wages. According to the A. F. of L. the average weekly wage of workers increased 8.9 per cent between March, 1933 and March, 1934; during the same period, food prices rose 20 per cent and clothing and furnishings 28.4 per cent. There were still 10,900,000 workers unemployed in March, 1934 and 10,616,000 in April, 1934, and these figures took no count of the young people, out of schools and colleges, who had never had jobs at all nor of white-collar workers. The amount expended from public funds for the direct relief of unemployed persons and the care of needy families was more than one-fifth larger in March, 1934 than in the previous months of maximum expenditure, March and November, 1933. On April 1, 1934, relief rolls were carrying 4,700,000 families, an all-time peak. In one hundred and forty cities and urban centers, the number of families on relief rose, between March and April, 1934, from 1,429,000 to 1,975,000, an increase of 38 per cent; relief expenditures in the same areas rose from $31,475,900 to $45,884,000, an increase of 46 per cent. Also, the farmer's position was not much better off. In April, 1934, the index of farm prices stood at 74, while the index

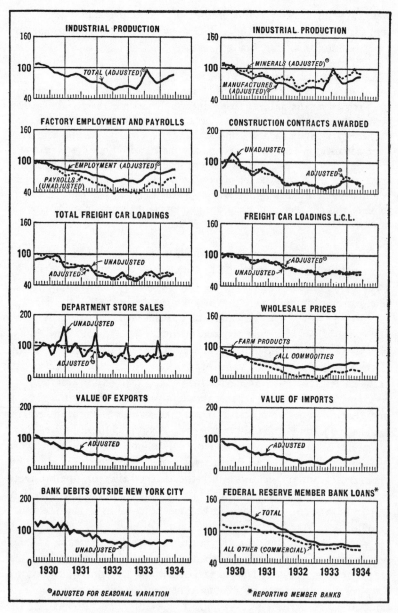

THE COURSE OF INDUSTRIAL RECOVERY

for prices paid by farmers had mounted to 120; thus the ratio of prices received by farmers to prices paid out for commodities needed was 62 in April, 1934.

Financial operations did not warrant too much optimism. The following figures, based on returns submitted by reporting member banks of the Federal Reserve system in 91 leading cities, show the changes that had occurred between May 3, 1933 and May 2, 1934 (figures in millions of dollars): [2]

	As of May 2, 1934	Change from May 3, 1933
Loans on securities	$ 3,577	—$ 121
All other loans	4,559	— 147
Investments in U. S. government bonds	6,255	+ 1,346
Reserves	2,588	+ 1,124
Deposits		
Demand	12,221	+ 1,873
Time	4,454	+ 124
Government	1,055	+ 797

The *New Republic's* discussion of these figures is illuminating:

Loans on securities are off $121,000,000 for the year. (These are by no means all for margin gambling; many firms finance their current needs by borrowing on securities in their possession.) "All other" loans, chiefly commercial paper, the financial life blood of commerce, are off $147,000,000 from a year ago, off more than two billions from April, 1932, and off $3,400,000,000 from April, 1931. Against this the increases are in two places only, investments in government bonds and excess reserves. Spending government money has its consequences, but the paper bond held by the bank means nothing in itself. Excess reserves are, if possible, even more idle so far as commerce is concerned. What has happened is essentially simple. The government has spent vast sums. The receipt for those sums, the bonds, are in the hands of the banks and show in the table. The money itself, the purchasing power put out by government spending, has promptly flowed back to the banks, which, having no use for it, keep it in the form of excess reserves, there to appear again in the table. The circle is closed, the government's money has stopped flowing.

Also, long-term loans, that is to say the flotation of capital issues,

[2] From *New Republic*, May 23, 1934.

showed no real gains. In the year 1933, a total of $722,000,000 in new issues was sold as compared with $1,165,000,000 in 1932, $6,909,000,000 in 1930 and $10,091,000,000 in 1929. (Of these totals, but $160,000,000 was for private enterprise in 1933, as compared with $325,000,000 in 1932, $4,483,000,000 in 1930, and $8,002,000,000 in 1929.) During the four months, January–April, 1934, the total of new capital issues was $367,000,000; this was not very much greater than the total for the four months, April–July, 1933, which was $308,000,000. The flotations for private enterprise, however, were considerably smaller, being $62,000,000 in the four months of 1934 as compared with $86,000,000 in the four months of 1933. In June, 1934, of the total new capital issues of $123,000,000, all but $9,000,000 were floated by states and municipalities.

The picture was not one of unmitigated gloom, at any rate as far as profits were concerned. According to the National City Bank, the combined net profits, less deficits, of 1,475 companies showed a 2.6 per cent rate of return upon net worth in 1933 as contrasted with a net deficit in 1932. At the beginning of 1932, the aggregate net worth of these companies had been $27,367,000,000 and the combined deficit for the year had been $97,000,000; in 1933 their net worth was $24,962,000,000 and their combined profits $661,-000,000. The trend was continuing into 1934, for the first 250 companies to report their earnings for the first half-year of 1934 showed net profits of $276,653,000 as compared with $86,362,000 for the same period of 1933.

Undoubtedly, it was difficult to cast up accounts a year or so after the New Deal's inception. Psychologically, a decided improvement had evidenced itself in the temper of the country: the black despair of a year before had been turned into a fair degree of confidence at any rate, as far as the business community was concerned; there still was evident a willingness on the part of a large section of the population to trust the President implicitly. Surely the President would yet produce a working plan! There was a good deal of debate over the character of the changes being effected. The Baltimore *Sun* characterized the Administration's program as "a catch-all of alluring theories superficially advanced and superficially accepted"; to the New York *World-Telegram*, on the other hand, it was a new "political method, the method of planned experiment." Certain institutional advances had taken place: unfair competitive practices had been largely curbed; child labor had been abolished in many industries; sweatshop labor had been cut down; daily hours of work had been reduced and more leisure time (for those who were employed and therefore had funds to profit thereby) had been created. The government itself, through a bewildering number of agencies and devices, had labored heroically to release new credits and thus start again the life blood pumping through the veins of private activity.

However, as was indicated above, not only was the general picture none too reassuring but there were particular aspects of recovery over which the discerning had reason to shake their heads. The capital goods industries, upon which the health of business enterprise in America really depended, were lagging behind seriously. (It has been estimated that the industries producing capital goods represented about half of the country's productive capacity and that in 1929 the total production of capital goods amounted to about $40,000,000,000 as against $30,000,000,000 in consumers' goods.) With the capital goods industries in depression, and because of this with some 6,000,000 industrial workers among the unemployable, the buying power available for consumers' goods was definitely limited. The following table shows that the improvement in some of the more important of the capital goods industries had not been very significant. (Index numbers of the Federal Reserve Board for industrial production adjusted for seasonal variation, 1923–25 average = 100.)

	May, 1933	May, 1934
Iron and steel	49	85
Lumber	30	33
Automobiles	50	78
Shipbuilding	25	65 *
Cement	42	57
Zinc	45	65
Lead	37	66

* April, 1934.

Nothing was more unsettling to the New Deal than the drought and hot weather which scorched the agricultural sections of the country in the late spring and the midsummer of 1934. Centering first in the Dakotas and Minnesota the drought moved through the Middle West and the Central South, leaving no important growing area untouched. The effect on crops and livestock was dismaying. The corn yield was estimated at 1,607,000,000 bushels on August 10, as compared with 2,344,000,000 bushels for the year previous; wheat production was placed at 491,000,000 bushels, as compared with 528,000,000 bushels for the year before; the cotton forecast was the lowest in a generation, being 9,195,000 bales, as compared with 13,047,000 bales in 1933. The Department of Agriculture anticipated that production of oats, barley, flaxseed, and buckwheat, in addition to corn and wheat, would be the smallest in thirty years or more; the hay and tobacco crops also were seriously affected; the government was compelled to buy up 2,600,000 head of cattle for slaughter because of the parching of wide belts of pasturing areas. The estimated damage was $5,000,000,000; some 5,300,000 people were involved; hundreds of thousands of persons were already destitute and being supported by federal relief.

The results of the drought one could only guess at. It was possible that some farmers, lucky enough to be out of the blighted regions and still in possession of their crops, would benefit because of climbing prices; probably an equally large number, however, were totally ruined. Again, carryovers, which before had acted as checks on inordinate price increases, were being reduced to normal (as in the case of cotton) or totally wiped out (as in the case of grains). There was a very real danger of sharp price rises and therefore increases in the cost of living for urban consumers, rises which wages would not find it possible to absorb. Thus, on August 8, cotton was selling at 14 cents on the exchanges; hogs were bringing $5.35 a hundredweight; grains attained their peaks for the year, while butter, eggs, and potatoes moved up as well. In the Northwest, retail prices of foodstuffs in the cities had already advanced an average of 12 per cent, by the first week in August. Put generally, it was doubtful whether the farmers, by and large, were likely to profit from the elimination of the agricultural surpluses; on the other hand, the working populations would no doubt feel the weight of higher living costs, thus adding to their restiveness. Whether, in view of Nature's ironic trick, the Department of Agriculture could resist the pressure to force the abandonment of the restriction program, on which its whole theory for coping with agriculture's decline was based, remained to be seen.

Agriculture was apparently in permanent depression; there appeared to be small hope of reviving the country's foreign trade; monopoly had raised its head to stifle small business enterprise and to control prices; labor thwarted of its right to organize and bargain collectively had become intransigent and was using the strike weapon more and more frequently and with growing militancy. To the development of these aspects of the New Deal in practice we must now turn.

The Failure of Voluntary Acreage Reduction

The Administration's program for recovery in agriculture, by means of voluntary acreage reduction, began to meet with insuperable obstacles almost from the very start. As we have seen, acreage, according to the specifications of the AAA, was cut and the huge subsidies in the form of rental or benefit payments largely (which came out of the pockets of the consumers) were paid; but the Administration quickly found that acreage reduction was not synonymous with yield reduction and that higher farm prices did not necessarily imply increased agricultural purchasing power.

The case of cotton, while not entirely typical, is illuminating. The plow-up campaign of 1933 eliminated fully one-fourth of the acreage under cultivation, reducing the growing crop's area from 41,000,000 to 30,000,000 acres. But the weather was kind—and cotton growers had been resourceful. Thanks to intensive cultivation and the use of fertilizer, the yield per acre, which for the preceding five-year period had average 174 pounds, increased to over 209 pounds. The year's crop was 13,177,000 bales; it was equal to that of 1932; and the carryover of 11,500,000 bales was cut down only slightly. As might have been expected, talk of drastic reduction in the United States encouraged growers in other areas to increase their plantings; as a result, the total of foreign cotton production reached the highest figure since the pre-depression season of 1928–29, plans were made for the opening of new cotton regions in Africa and India, and the world position of American cotton was worse than ever before. In corn and hogs the net effects were not very different. As for the purchasing power of farmers, it has already been pointed out that all hopes for parity for agriculture had got nowhere: whereas, in May, 1933, the month

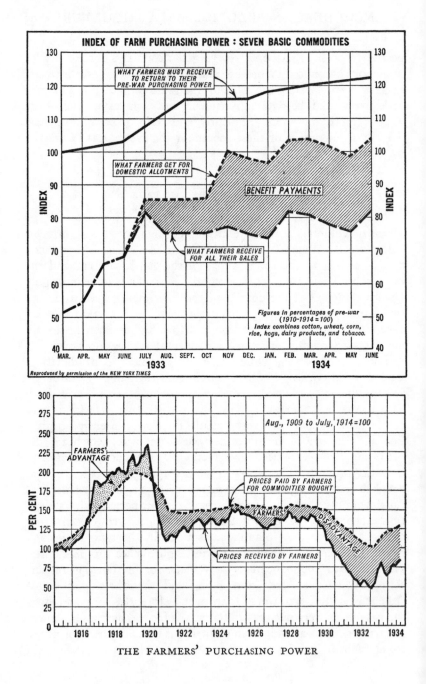

THE FARMERS' PURCHASING POWER

that the AAA was established, the farmer's dollar, in terms of purchasing power, had been worth 61 cents, in May, 1934, a whole year later, it was still worth only 61 cents.

Reduction of acreage, which had cost the American consumer through the processing taxes at least $150,000,000 in 1933, and was to· cost more than $1,000,000,000 additional in 1934, had failed. By the end of one year's experimenting, the New Dealers in agriculture were confessing that the plan could not have the desired result of eliminating surpluses and, therefore, raising the real income of farmers. These had been some of the immediate effects of attempted curtailment of the more important cash crops. Intensive cultivation of acreage without any decrease in production had resulted, as in cotton. Many farmers had refused to join in the sign-up campaign, hoping to benefit from the reductions of their fellow-growers. (This had happened in the case of winter wheat plantings for 1934, where only half of the sought-for reduction had been pledged.) Consumer resistance set in. (This had occurred in the case of hog products so that, despite the slaughter of young pigs and sows, prices did not advance materially; indeed, many farmers were reporting that the packers were requiring the payment of the processing taxes by the farmers themselves.) Farmers began to shift to uncontrolled crops, resulting in increases in production among those articles for which subsidies were not being paid. (So marked had this movement become that in March, 1934, as was pointed out above, Congress was compelled to pass a measure extending the benefits of subsidies to beef and dairy cattle, peanuts, rye, barley, flax, and grain sorghum.)

The complete regimentation of agriculture seemed the only way out. The approval of the Cotton Control Act (the so-called Bankhead bill) on April 21, 1934, indicated that the Administration's agricultural policy was to be based on the forced reduction of the surpluses through the licensing of every individual farmer. The Cotton Control measure, whose methods it reasonably could be expected would be applied to the other cash crops, embodied the following: for the crop year 1934–35 production of cotton was to be limited to 10,000,000 bales; the plan might be extended by the President for an additional year provided two-thirds of the cotton growers gave their consent; all cotton-growing states, on the basis of their yields over the previous five years, were to be allotted quotas; quotas, in turn, were to be fixed for counties and

then for individual farmers, the latter receiving tax-exemption certificates, or licenses, for the amounts allotted to them (and, of
course, benefit payments); production in excess of the stipulated
amounts was to be taxed at the gins at the rate of 50 per cent of
the average central market price, but not less than 5 cents per
pound; the Secretary of Agriculture, who was to administer the
act, was to have the right to prohibit the raising of other cash crops
on cotton acreage withdrawn from cultivation. In the last day of
its session, on June 18, 1934, Congress passed the Tobacco Control Act, which imposed a somewhat similar quota system on tobacco planters. Under the act, growers signing up for production
control agreed to reduce the 1934 crop by about 30 per cent. All
those who did not sign up were to be penalized through the imposition of an ad valorem tax of not less than 25 per cent nor more
than 33⅓ per cent. The plan was to be continued for the 1935
crop if three-fourths of the growers approved.

What did this mean? It was a definite step in the direction of
that complete governmental control against which Secretary Wallace himself had protested in his pamphlet "America Must
Choose," published a short two months before the enactment of
the Bankhead bill. The Secretary had said:

If we finally go all the way toward nationalism, it may be necessary
to have compulsory control of marketing, licensing of plowed lands, and
base and surplus quotas for every farmer for every product for each
month in the year. . . . It may be necessary to make a public utility
out of agriculture and apply to it a combination of an Esch-Cummins
Act and an Adamson Act. Every plowed field would have its permit
sticking up on its post.

The economic implications of the step were even more significant. The Cotton Control and Tobacco Control laws implied, in effect, the licensing and, therefore, the continuance in production of
every grower of a cash cotton or tobacco crop who had previously
participated in commercial agriculture; in short, in the case of
cotton, the licensing on a pro rata, farm for farm basis, of every
one of the 1,600,000 farmers, whether he was efficient or not,
whether he cultivated submarginal lands or not, whether he used
or was in a position to employ technical and mechanical methods
in his operations. Clearly, licensing of all farmers was bound to

have but one result: the destruction of agriculture's efficiency by the government itself.

No better witness against such a program of reduction can be presented than Mr. Wallace himself. In his annual report for 1933 he had said:

A temporary and varying reduction in the productive acreage [of each farm] seriously disturbs the farm economy; it may modify established rotations and feeding practices; . . . and it necessitates the disuse or less effective use of the labor, machinery, work stock, and the equipment required to farm larger acreages. Overhead costs frequently cannot be curtailed in proportion to the reduction in farm operations.

WERE THE HOPES FOR THE REVIVAL OF FOREIGN TRADE ILLUSORY?

The price of recovery in agriculture, apparently, was to be this: farmers, in the face of all they had been taught by public agencies over fifty years, were to be encouraged to unlearn their lessons in plant and animal breeding, animal husbandry, the use of machinery and fertilizers, the practices of rotation, and revert to the primitive, slipshod technics of an older day. But if the immediate program for agriculture had vital flaws in it, surely the New Dealers had prepared plans for permanent reform? They had; and the United States was asked to consider two programs, the first calling for our orderly return to foreign markets by means of the route of reciprocal trading agreements, and the second for the retirement from commercial production of America's submarginal farmers and their settlement on subsistence homesteads. It has already been pointed out how Secretary Wallace addressed himself to the question of the restoration of foreign trade in his pamphlet, "America Must Choose."

The Secretary to the contrary notwithstanding, one may doubt if agriculture will derive any real benefits from a revival of foreign trade. It must be apparent that reciprocal agreements, as far as we are concerned, can be reached most easily with those nations which are prepared to import our capital goods, that is to say, the more backward industrial lands of the world. We can quickly dispose of railroad equipment, ships, machine tools, automobiles and trucks, agricultural machinery, and building materials to countries like Russia, Argentina, Chile, and China; but what can we take in return? Russia's leading surplus commodities are oil, fur skins, cereals and lumber; Argentina's are wheat, meats, hides, wool, and flax seed; China's are furs, soy beans and bean cake, vegetable oils, tea, cotton yarn and goods, and silk; Chile's are copper, nitrates, wool, and wheat. The great proportion of the enumerated articles are raw materials, many are agricultural goods, virtually all we ourselves produce in excess of domestic needs.

It is difficult to see how oversea markets for our surplus crops can be revived, short of giving the crops away. Europe may definitely be left out of the reckoning: European nations will not buy our foodstuffs as long as the danger of war threatens and the need for building up reactionary rural blocs against revolutionary proletarian threat continues. South America is no market, for the countries of that continent produce surplus agricultural products. The Orient remains. We can sell tobacco, wheat, and cotton to Chinese, Malayans, and Siamese: teaching these peoples to consume wheat instead of rice, thereby ruining the rice growers of India and Indo-China; encouraging the development of native cotton-goods industries, to the harm of our own factories: but we can buy little from those lands in return. We can, of course, accept their silver, to be piled up in Treasury vaults for safe keeping: and this, of course, is quite a likely possibility. But none but a silver mine owner would look upon this device as a permanent method of agricultural reform.

The vesting in the President of executive powers to raise and lower tariffs, as a means of forcing reciprocal treaties, was, of course, a powerful weapon and might in the long run do some good. Its edge, however, had been dulled somewhat by Congressional limitation and governmental policy; thus, Congress had written into the Reciprocal Tariff Act a prohibition against any agreement to "reduce in any manner any of the indebtedness of any foreign power" (referring, of course, to the war debts); the State Department was committed to the preservation of the most-favored-nation principle; while President Roosevelt himself had given a pledge that "no sound and important American interest will be injuriously disturbed" by concessions made to foreign importers.

True, there still was left considerable room for tariff bargaining. According to the Foreign Policy Association, which based its findings on the investigations of the Tariff Commission, there were upwards of one thousand foreign articles on which duties might be lowered and which therefore could be used as the basis for reciprocal treaties. The Foreign Policy Association found that these articles fell into the following groups: (1) imports which were essentially non-competitive, because we had no domestic production in these fields; (2) those which were completely or almost completely excluded, that is, where the importations represented less than 5 per cent of domestic consumption; (3) those on which abnormally high rates of duty, especially those over 50 per cent ad valorem, were imposed; (4) those which have been substantially curtailed in recent years as compared with our domestic needs; and (5) those on which protective duties have been in effect for a considerable time, without having stimulated a substantial increase in domestic production.

There is one doubt that must be raised. In view of the long conditioning American industry has had in a protective tariff environment, a sudden change to an international unfavorable balance situation under which the United States would import more than it would export—and particularly buy from abroad manufactured goods—is unlikely. If the question is seriously considered in all its ramifications, there is a greater possibility of the bars being let down for the importation of foreign raw materials and foodstuffs than for the importation of finished goods. Indeed, at a meeting of the representatives of organized farmers, held at Washington in April, 1934, exactly this suspicion was voiced again and again. Speakers pointed to the refusal of the Treasury Department to maintain an anti-dumping order against rye grain from Poland, to the State Department's leniency as regards agricultural quarantine matters, to the opposition of the State and War Departments to the taxes on foreign vegetable and fish oils, and to Roosevelt's willingness to admit into the country sheep and lambs from Patagonia. According to the newspaper report of the meeting, members present expressed themselves as follows:

We are appreciative of the President's keen interest in the welfare of agriculture, but frankly we are afraid of the State Department, in which department we know practically all of the work of negotiating reciprocal trade agreements will be done. Those who are informed about

Washington matters know that whenever the State Department gets up against agricultural matters, something slips. We have seen it in quarantine and many other instances.

THE DREAM OF SUBSISTENCE HOMESTEADS

Undoubtedly, the plan for the establishment of "a neighborhood of trade" (as Secretary Wallace called the reciprocal trading idea) had in it qualities of wishful thinking; as a long-time reform program, it was difficult to see how it could effect anything but the doom of American agriculture. The Administration's other long-time proposal for agriculture's reconstruction, that of the creation of innumerable communities of subsistence homesteads, took on some of the aspects of fantasy.

In 1929, out of the total of 6,000,000 farmers in the United States, there were almost 3,000,000 whose average annual income, from the sale of cash crops, was not more than $356. These 3,000,000 farmers had to spend among them for taxes, mortgage payments, improvements of their plants and operations, as well as for household goods, clothing, and all those many little comforts and luxuries which machine production presumably had put within the reach of the humblest, the sum of $1,041,517,000. The other 3,000,000 farmers had cash incomes, from sale of crops, of $8,570,000,000. Thus, a little more than 50 per cent of the farmers of the United States produced almost 90 per cent of the value of the country's commercial crops. If natural forces were permitted to operate—a free market, the growing pressure of fixed charges, foreclosure, and bankruptcy—many of the 3,000,000 small and inefficient farmers would be driven off their holdings and added to the industrial unemployed. But there were already from 11,000,000 to 15,000,000 unemployed persons on the bread-lines and relief rolls of our cities. Obviously, the submarginal farmer must be kept on the land; obviously, also, out of commercial production.

This is the background of the romantic vision to which the Administration gave the name "subsistence homesteads." Doomed farmers, who operated at a low order of efficiency, were to be moved out of their isolated little islands, whether in the cut-over regions of the Great Lakes States, the piney-woods and sand-hills areas of the Atlantic coastal plain country, the Appalachian highlands districts, the arid stretches at the edge of the Great Plains, and transplanted to semi-rural villages. Here they were to be settled in model communities, on plots ranging from five to forty acres, where they could grow crops for home consumption only and revive the ancient handicrafts of spinning, weaving, wood working, pottery making, and similar pursuits of a contented peasantry. To provide cash—to pay for the social services and the little amenities of life (after all, the radio and automobile, cosmetics and silk stockings, books and the movies are some of the fruits of our modern civilization)—work was to be provided in factories which, on so many magic carpets, would be conveniently whisked to these little modern Arcadias.

The happy results envisaged by proponents of the scheme were many: the surpluses of agricultural goods would be eliminated; more people would live in semi-rural surroundings, at the same time learning to cultivate again a pioneering independence; a long step would be taken toward the decentralization of industry and the reduction of many of those social ills which have flourished with the growth of great cities. Assistant Secretary of Agriculture Tugwell, in particular, became the defender of the new peasantry that was to be established; while Emergency Relief Administrator Hopkins was able to see subsistence homesteads not only as retreats for America's surplus farmers but for its surplus industrial workers as well. Despite a good deal of public enthusiasm at Washington, however, the subsistence homesteads continued to remain in the "demonstration" stage.

Under the second title of the NIRA, the sum of $25,000,000 was granted to the President "for making loans for and otherwise aiding in the purchase of subsistence homesteads." The President entrusted the carrying out of this program to the Secretary of the Interior, who, in turn, created in his Department the Division of Subsistence Homesteads with an advisory committee to stand by. On September 26, 1933, the advisory committee assembled and presented a series of recommendations, of which the more significant were the following. The fund of $25,000,000 was to be used to set up "demonstration projects which will point the way to a program of a permanent character." The projects were to be organized and administered through local non-profit or limited-dividend corporations to which the federal funds were to be lent. These loans were to be made at an interest rate of 3 per cent and amortized over a period not to exceed thirty years; initial payments might be deferred, but deferment was not to exceed two years. Individual plots could be either leased or sold to the homesteaders. Adequate agricultural and other advice and guidance were to be assured the homesteaders. Subsequently, it was decided to set up a subsidiary federal corporation which was to enter into contracts of sale directly with the homesteaders. Also, loans for the purchase of equipment, tools and machinery, live stock, trees, fertilizer, etc. were to be granted if these were unobtainable from other sources. It will be noted that no provision was made for the establishment of factories in these homestead areas.

M. L. Wilson, who was made director of the division, announced that the projects would consist of five major types, as follows: (1) Workers' garden homesteads located near small industrial centers, where industry may be said already to be decentralized. (2) Workers' garden homesteads near large industrial centers, where heavy industries not likely to lend themselves to decentralization were located. (3) Projects for the rehabilitation of stranded industrial groups, largely miners of whom there were probably 200,000. (4) Projects involving the rehabilitation of farmers engaged on lands submarginal for agriculture. (5) Movement of population, largely farm families, from submarginal dry-farming lands in the West to unoccupied farms on existing federal reclamation projects.

The communities of homesteaders were to consist of from twenty-five to one hundred families, the average family plot running from one to five acres. In rural reconstruction projects the size of the individual holding was to be larger "and agricultural operations somewhat more extensive in scope." It was estimated that the homesteads would cost their occupants from $2,000 to $3,000; on the basis of plans already announced, $2,500 apparently was to be the average cost, to be amortized over twenty years. In some cases a down payment was to be collected; in one instance, it was as high as $500 per family. At an average cost of $2,500 per family, it can be seen that the total of $25,000,000 allotted for the purpose could provide for but 10,000 families.

The earliest approved projects included the following: the settlements in Jasper and Putnam counties, Ga., at a cost of $1,000,-000, of 500 farming families who had been living on eroded submarginal lands; in Pender county, N. C., also at a cost of $1,-

000,000, of from 300 to 400 families made up of submarginal farmers and unemployed industrial workers; at Birmingham, Ala., at a cost of $750,000, of 300 families whose breadwinners worked in the steel mills; at Reedsville, W. Va., at a cost not yet determined, of 200 families of stranded coal miners; at Decatur, Ind., at a cost of $125,000, of 40 to 48 families working in small diversified industries at low incomes; in Monmouth county, N. J., at a cost of $500,000, of 200 Jewish families from the congested clothing centers of New York City, Newark, Jersey City, and Philadelphia; in northern Wisconsin, at a cost of $750,000, of 400 families, made up of isolated farmers living in cut-over forest regions, who were to combine work in forestry with part-time farming.

But what of occasional jobs to provide the cash required for payments on homesteads and for taxes, house furnishings, clothing, the radio, and automobile? It is true that in some of the demonstration projects homesteaders were to be located near large cities or national forests; this, obviously, could not be regarded as the solution for all the submarginal farmers and unemployable industrial workers who were to be transplanted. Factories would have to be erected, either by private capital or from public funds. In only one project, that of the colony of Jewish needle trade workers in New Jersey, had definite assurances of the establishment of a factory been received; and in this case the funds were to be supplied partly by a private group, partly out of philanthropic contributions, and partly out of the original down payment of $500 each homesteader was to be expected to make.

In the case of the Reedsville, W. Va. project, the original plan had called for the building by the federal government of a $500,-000 factory to manufacture furniture for the Post Office Department. The grant, however, had met with stubborn resistance in the House of Representatives and had twice failed of approval, largely because the furniture industry had pointed out—with entire justice—that it was operating at only 20 per cent of capacity and that plants capable of supplying Post Office equipment were everywhere standing idle in neighboring states. This initial check to the Administration's willingness to dip into the Treasury in order to locate an industrial plant in the midst of a subsistence homestead colony indicated that there would be no easy sailing for such a program on a wholesale scale.

It must be apparent that the transplanting of large groups of submarginal farmers is such a vast and costly program that only the romantic can regard its implications without blinking. It has already been indicated that it will cost at least $2,500 a family to resettle homesteaders in the new village communities. The problem of the farm surplus will not even be touched unless at least one million rural families are taken out of commercial agriculture and put upon a self-sufficing basis; and relocating them alone would cost $2,500,000,000. This, of course, makes not the slightest provision for the creation of part-time employment without which these families would be as hopelessly marooned economically as many now are. It is difficult to see why private capital should move at the behest of the federal government; but assuming that in one-half the cases private funds would be attracted by a cheap labor supply and other advantages government financing would again be necessary. On the basis of the Reedsville, W. Va. estimate, $2,500 per family would be required for capital expenditures; this would add another $1,250,000,000 to the cost. To take all our three million surplus farmers off the land—not to speak of the surplus industrial workers—and to establish them in an economy where they could expect to live a little above the meager levels they today endure would, therefore, cost the federal government in excess of $10,000,000,000.

Ten billions of dollars merely to create a sheltered peasantry, and to move three million American farming families from their present wretched condition to some future uncertainty! And who pays the piper: for the establishment of these new little isles of content; for their equipment and repair? Who will pay for the roads and the schoolhouses and the public buildings and the poor houses and the old age pensions and the support of dependent children and the health services, while the homesteaders, for want of other beguilement, work away at their arts and crafts? On whom will the burden of taxation fall to support a thousand-odd Brook Farms: on whom else but the shoulders of the industrial workers and the remaining commercial farmers?

Other embarrassing doubts obtrude. Something, of course, will have to be done about the many service activities which, in the course of time, have grown up about the settlements to be wiped out: the local hay and feed establishments, the grocery shops, the professional men's offices, the schools and court houses. To the bill, obviously, will have to be added the cost of compensating all those humbler members of the middle class who once served the farmers and who, in turn, will be doomed now that these farmers are to be transported to happier seats; to the bill, also, will have to be added the cost of financial assistance to be rendered those townships and counties which will become crippled as a result of the departure of so many of their property-owners and taxpayers.

Again, the creation of such a large peasant class, with next to no cash incomes and receiving the benefit of "vocational guidance," must undoubtedly contract the size of the domestic market for capital goods and consumers' goods. People who will have plenty of time and no financial worries, so that they can grow their own flax and weave their own linen, card their own wool and make their own homespun, tan their own hides and put together their own rude shoes, will not need store clothes. Or, for that matter, machinery, iron and steel products, chemicals, and those thousand and one other articles upon whose mass consumption our industrial civilization depends. If all this is likely to depress the lot of the industrial workers, the direct cheap competition of the homesteaders, at the mercy of what local employment conditions they may find in such factories as may be erected in their colonies, will produce further unhappy effects. Urban labor, at least, has collective strength and mobility with which to fight intolerable working conditions; with these weapons it is in a position to improve its wages and hours of work. But a soil-bound peasantry, isolated in rural communities and dependent upon a little cash to meet its fixed charges, must accept whatever labor terms are offered. Such cheap wages of labor cannot but have their repercussions elsewhere, particularly when the goods fabricated compete with the products of industrial labor.

The commercial farmers, also, will suffer in a variety of ways. Their market will be contracted because a peasantry producing its own food, feedstuffs, and fibers will not have any need for the wares of the wheat, corn, and cotton growers; and they will have the competition—in increasing roadside stands and bootleg operations at city markets and dairies—of a great number of favored peasants who will be in a position to sell for whatever their goods will bring. The experiment with nation-wide prohibition should have taught us the impossibility of coping with the petty cheatings of a population once it has decided against observing an unpopular law. How to make self-sufficing homesteaders grow only enough for their own needs will be a neat administrative problem for another generation of New Dealers to handle.

Finally, it is idle to believe that we can expect decentralization of industry—that other great benefit to be derived from subsistence homesteads—merely by decree. The location of plants is a complex, following fairly well-defined economic laws. Industrial establishments are located where they are because of nearness either to raw materials or to consumption markets or to a labor supply or to fuel resources, or any of these factors in combination; favorable public policies as regards taxation and factory legislation also play their parts. Industry, naturally, will not decentralize at the request of government but will obey the laws of its own particular development. It may be assumed that such factories as are erected in conjunction with homestead village projects will have to be in large part government establishments. At a stage in capitalism's development, where its outstanding problem is excess plant capacity, to engage in further plant expansion—at the taxpayer's expense—is to make confusion worse confounded.

It is not difficult to assemble innumerable political, social, and economic arguments against the fantastic device of subsistence homesteads. Yet—who knows?—it may be that an American government, hard driven by the contradictions of its own position, may even (as in Italy and Germany) seek to build up exactly such a sheltered peasant group as a rural reactionary bloc to withstand the revolutionary demands of the organized industrial workers. When and if such a program on a wholesale scale is really embarked upon, then it will be possible to say that the United States has taken a definite step in the direction of a right dictatorship.

CAN AGRICULTURE BE SAVED?

The dilemma of American agriculture is that of our modern economy. There are too many farmers, just as there are too many industrial workers, because both agriculture and industry have become too efficient to operate in a system based on the profit motive. The problem of agriculture is further complicated by the existence of an inelastic home market: needs for foods and fibers cannot be expanded indefinitely as can those for other consumers' goods. In addition, our foreign customers have melted away and it is difficult to see, in the light of America's pressing necessity to find outlets for capital goods and savings and the need of other peoples to sell their agricultural surpluses, how they can be recaptured.

If we are to maintain our agriculture at the highest pitch of efficiency we cannot escape these conclusions: that we have too many farmers and too much land in cultivation. The problem of the surplus farmer, therefore, is the problem of our whole economic system. No idealization of homestead communities and handicrafts production can conceal the fact that such use of the land for the support of a peasant sustenance economy means turning back the clock fully a thousand years. On the other hand, if we really mean everything we say about living in an age of abundance, then we must preserve the great gains agriculture has won through technical and mechanical improvements and so order our life that room can be found elsewhere for the farmers who are no longer needed on the land. In the final analysis, we are confronted by this question: Can we provide for all our surplus farmers and all our surplus workers, at high consumption levels, in an economic order that is founded on profit and not on use? The New Deal's program for recovery and reform in agriculture, because in the first instance it is aimed at the destruction of agriculture's efficiency and in the second because it is based on a depressing of living standards for excess tillers of the soil, avoids an answer. And for this reason, the New Deal's plans for agriculture in the United States must be regarded as profoundly unsatisfactory.

V. THE NEW DEAL IN PRACTICE: IN INDUSTRY

THE GROWTH OF MONOPOLY

WHILE industry, during the initial months of the New Deal, gladly accepted public intervention and raised no objections to the Administration program, it soon became apparent that the truce between government and business—for it was not more than this—was to be of brief duration. As the economic processes began again to move, by the midsummer and fall of 1933, complaints began to pour in more and more of the violation of codes of fair competition by factory and store managers. Indeed, so widespread had the practice become that in a radio address on October 22, President Roosevelt was compelled to admonish "chiselers" that the penalties authorized by the laws would be imposed.

Serious in itself, this was not nearly as disquieting as the growing protest on the part of industrialists against the basic principles of the New Deal. Increasingly, spokesmen for business (and these were in time joined by leaders of the Republican party) began to demand that government retire again to its traditional functions and leave the operations of industrial affairs to private enterprise and the chances of the free market. Rashness itself characterized the remarks of many of these persons. Thus, the president of the National Industrial Conference Board, a research organization financed by large business groups, in a newspaper interview, insisted that the New Deal was socialism pure and simple and that the American revolution was "proceeding at a greater velocity than any previous transformation of a nation's economic structure; faster than Mussolini's, than Hitler's, or the Bolshevik rising in Russia."

The sometimes unguarded and often airily delivered statements of New Deal theoreticians were combed over carefully and given a much greater significance than was intended; and conservative critics could not read utterances like the following without already seeing the specter of the revolution approaching.

There is no choice presented to American business between intelligently planned and controlled industrial operations and a return to the gold-plated anarchy that masqueraded as rugged individualism. There is only the choice presented between private and public election of the directors of industry. If the privately elected boards of directors and the privately chosen managers of industry undertake their task and fulfill their responsibility, they will end all talk of dictatorships and governmental control of business. But if they hold back and waste these precious hours, if they take counsel with prejudice and doubt, if they fumble their great opportunity, they may suddenly find that it has gone forever. (Donald R. Richberg, General Counsel of the NRA, at New York on July 6, 1933.)

And those people who would have us crawl back to the old ideas, like a wounded animal to an abandoned den, misread the temper of the people as well as the intelligence of the present government. We are trying to show that heaped up corporate surpluses and the over-concentration of wealth are not the life of trade but the death of trade. Incomes must be transformed into larger wages and higher prices to farmers, not simply stacked up in sterile hoards of capital, if wealth in any large and gratifying sense is to breed again. (Rexford G. Tugwell, Assistant Secretary of Agriculture, at Chicago on October 29, 1933.)

It did not avail Mr. Tugwell, who was regarded as a leader of the Brain Trust, to protest that he did not believe in national planning, the transplanting of Russian methods here, or the adoption of governmental controls in violation of the Constitution: despite his insistence that he was a conservative (which, economically speaking, he really was), the Assistant Secretary of Agriculture was made the victim of a good deal of open misrepresentation and covert abuse. By the spring of 1934, so great had the hostility to his presence in Washington become, there was considerable difficulty in obtaining the Senate's confirmation of his promotion to the post of Undersecretary of Agriculture.

Other agencies were also at work. On October 15, 1933, Alfred E. Smith, who by now had openly identified himself with the forces of big business, laid down the first barrage for what turned out to be a concerted attack on the New Deal from the right, when he referred to it as the "heavy, cold, clammy hand of bureaucracy." He was immediately followed by the newspaper publishers Paul Block and William Randolph Hearst. Mr. Block, in a signed editorial in his own newspapers, which was reprinted widely as a paid advertisement, told Washington that it had not yet proved its capacity for running its own business; how then did it dare run the business of everyone else? "What industry needs from the Administration is encouragement and not hindrance, for nearly everyone can sense that business is right on the edge of an upward move, but too many 'cooks' or 'experts' are at present blocking the road," said Mr. Block. Mr. Hearst was even blunter. The New Deal was a "socialistic dictatorship"; and it was imposing "upon industry, struggling toward recovery, shorter hours and higher pay and greater employment and heavier burdens in every direction than industry, weakened by depression and only newly recovering, was able to bear." On November 1, Mr. Gerard Swope, president of the General Electric Company and at the time head of the Industrial Advisory Board of the NRA, launched industry's heavy drive when he proposed that the control of business be turned back to its own leaders and the functions of the NRA be vested in a privately conducted National Chamber of Commerce and Industry—under a shadowy government supervision. When H. I. Harriman, president of the United States Chamber of Commerce, and General Hugh S. Johnson, the National Recovery Administrator, gave the Swope plan their immediate blessing, it was no longer a secret that the New Deal was meeting with organized opposition from without and disaffection from within.

In June, 1934, big business was still of the same mind: it had no objection to the existence of the codes—nay, it was willing to continue the system after the expiration of the NRA—but it demanded that industry be permitted to take over the task of self-regulation at once. This was the opinion arrived at by a group of America's greatest industrialists, constituting the present and past members of the Industrial Advisory Board, after a series of meetings during June 16–18, 1934. The plan of self-regulation proposed included the establishment of maximum hours of work and minimum wages for labor, the prohibition of child labor, the elimination of unfair trade practices, the relief of technological unemployment, and the conservation of natural resources. Nothing was said of recognizing the workers' right to organize for collective bargaining or of preventing monopoly prices.

If this was disheartening, what was to be said of the growing conviction that the chief function of the NIRA and the code-making process had become exactly that fostering of cartelization, with consequent strangulation of competition and the establishment of monopoly prices, which industrial leaders were proposing to continue forever? The Consumers' Advisory Board of the NRA, after having examined at length the working-out of codes, in the beginning of 1934 pointed out that "wholesale prices were rising, retail prices were bound to go up, and the consumer demand must inevitably drop." It warned that "unless the standards for wages and hours are decidedly changed, the increases of wages and employment required by the codes lie mostly in the past . . . since inventories have been fairly well built up, the growth of payrolls is not likely to continue unless there is further growth of the final consuming market."

From every side evidences began to accumulate that prices definitely were falling out of line. The following figures, for example, were submitted by the Mail Order Association of America to prove the effect of monopoly price practices countenanced by a number of the more important codes.

INDEX OF PRICES UNDER NO CODE AS YET, OR CODES FREE FROM PRICE PROVISIONS				INDEX OF PRICES UNDER APPROVED CODES CONTAINING OPEN-PRICE PROVISIONS			
			Dec. 15,				Dec. 15,
1924	1926	1929	1933	1924	1926	1929	1933
108.2	100.0	88.2	82.7	101.2	100.0	90.2	111.2

INDEX OF PRICES UNDER APPROVED CODES CONTAINING OUTRIGHT PRICE-FIXING PROVISIONS				UNITED STATES DEPARTMENT OF LABOR (INDEX OF PRICES OF FARM PRODUCTS)	
			Dec. 15,		Dec. 16,
1924	1926	1929	1933	1926	1933
100.8	100.0	95.3	98.6	100.0	55.9

The Administration was not unaware of these tendencies and repeatedly and publicly exhorted manufacturers and distributors to check too sudden price rises. Thus, General Johnson, in addressing a group of retail merchants, on January 18, 1934, pleaded: "Keep prices down—for God's sake, keep prices down. That and that alone is the royal road to recovery." While the President, before the assembled Code Authorities, on March 5, 1934, said: "With millions still unemployed, the power of our people to purchase and use the products of industry is still greatly curtailed. It can be increased and sustained only by striving for the lowest schedule of prices on which higher wages and increasing employment can be maintained." All this, however, was unavailing, and the real earnings of farmers and workers continued to decline. The redistribution of national income, which had been one of the major theoretical objectives of the New Deal, was as remote as ever before.

Support for the charge of the growth of monopoly, not only as regards price fixing but also as including limitation of productive capacity and output, allocation of quotas to inefficient plants, and excessive overhead costs—in fine, all the devices with which cartelization was associated—came from two governmental agencies. The Federal Trade Commission, in March, 1934, after having examined the operations of the iron and steel code, reported to the Senate that the monopoly practices against which it had frequently inveighed were if anything strengthened under the new dispensation. Specifically, it called attention to the fact that policies of the Iron and Steel Institute, the Code Authority for the industry, were dominated by the two or three great companies in the field, that price increases and price fixing had immediately been inaugurated, and that the iron and steel manufacturers were using the code to legalize practices which the commission had previously outlawed as opposed to the maintenance of fair competition. In particular, the Federal Trade Commission pointed to the restoration of basing-point prices which had been banned by its order in the Pittsburgh-plus case of 1924.

The whole controversy came to a head with the belated release of the initial reports of the National Recovery Review Board on May 21, 1934. (These had been submitted to the President on May 4.) This board, largely on the basis of the representations of Senators Borah and Nye that the codes were driving small enterprisers out of business, had been created on February 19, 1934, to hold hearings and collect evidences of repression; the veteran lawyer Clarence S. Darrow had been named its chairman. After having examined the work of Code Authorities in iron and steel, motion pictures, electrical goods, bituminous coal, and a number of lesser industries, the National Recovery Review Board came to

the conclusion that the NRA was fostering monopoly and op-
pressing small industrialists and distributors, that certain codes
were openly being administered by monopoly interests, and that
prices to consumers were at the mercy of monopoly control. The
board confirmed the opinion of the Federal Trade Commission
concerning the iron and steel code when it said of the Iron and
Steel Institute: "We have here a body not only perfectly equipped
to exercise monopolistic control, but . . . endowed with extraordinary powers incompatible with the ideals heretofore entertained
in a free country."

More sensational than these findings, which by this time were
generally suspected, was the supplementary report to the first report signed by Mr. Darrow and Mr. W. O. Thompson. (It was
subsequently revealed that the latter had written the statement.)
It reiterated charges of monopoly, called for transfer of code enforcement and fact finding from the NRA to the Federal Trade
Commission, and insisted that competition no longer could be re-
lied upon to protect the consumer. After having neatly summarized
the economics of monopoly operation, with its tendencies to lower
production costs (and therefore the wages of labor), eliminate
competition, and force up prices, the report ruled out a return to
small units in industry as impossible "in a situation where technological advance has produced a surplus." Said the report: "Only
by the fullest use of productive capacity for the raising of standards
of living of individuals and the community can a steady balance
be achieved in an age of abundance." The conclusion was therefore inescapable:

The choice is between monopoly sustained by government, which
is clearly the trend in the National Recovery Administration, and a
planned economy, which demands socialized ownership and control,
since only by collective ownership can the inevitable conflict of sep-
arately owned units for the market be eliminated in favor of planned
production. There is no hope for the small business man or for complete recovery in America in enforced restriction upon production
for the purpose of maintaining higher prices. The hope for the American people, including the small business man, not to be overwhelmed
by their own abundance lies in the planned use of America's resources
following socialization. To give the sanction of government to sustain
profits is not a planned economy, but a regimented organization for
exploitation.

While the NRA issued heated general and specific denials and even succeeded in persuading Roosevelt to dissolve the board [1] it must have been impressed by the favorable reception the report received; for on June 7, General Johnson declared that the policy of price-fixing in codes was to be drastically changed. Destructive price cutting was to be prohibited; minimum prices might be fixed only in "cases of demonstrable emergency"; and sales below cost of production were to be prohibited unless such prices were authorized by the NRA Administrator. Open-price posting would be tolerated only on condition that prices be reported to a neutral, confidential agency and the waiting periods be eliminated. Also, agreements to fix and maintain price terms or coercion to compel changes in price terms was to be regarded as in violation of the codes. When industrialists protested in dismay that complex trade practices would have to be revised overnight with resulting great disorganization, the General modified his order to apply only to pending codes and codes subsequently submitted for approval. As to codes already in force (and there were 450 such, which included nearly all the major industries), it was merely the General's hope "that Code Authorities of the approved codes will desire to agree" to the changed price policy. Obviously, the victory of the reformers had turned out to be a hollow one.

One year after the passage of the NIRA many observers were agreeing that the codes had succeeded in hastening the processes of monopoly growth in the United States. The following thoughtful analysis of George Soule was indeed difficult to confute:

And we have, in this country, an effort to turn the government of industry over to trade associations and the like, the main preoccupation of which seems to be to limit productive capacity, to restrict output, and to maintain prices. I do not know of any association of business competitors, whether called pool, cartel or institute, either now or in the past, which has concentrated its effort on enlarging production and reducing prices. Rather, such associations tend to keep prices up to the point which will allow the less efficient producers to make a profit. There are many signs that business in the United States is

[1] The National Recovery Review Board went out of existence June 30, 1934. Its third and final report, in which its general charges concerning monopolist practices were repeated, was released the next day. On July 14, 1934, it was announced that a new agency, the Industrial Appeals Board, had been established to act on complaints of inequitable application of NRA codes. It was assumed that the new board would pay particular attention to the grievances of small business men.

now organizing, under relaxation of the anti-trust laws, as it attempted to organize while they were still in force, and did so organize in some cases with success, to practice what Thorstein Veblen so aptly called "the conscientious withdrawal of efficiency."

Labor's Growing Militancy

Section 7 (a) of the NIRA, with its presumable promises of the right of collective bargaining, the free choice by workers of their own representatives, and their recognition by industry, was regarded by labor as a new charter of liberties; and the wage earners of the country, seizing the opportunity, flocked to join unions affiliated with the American Federation of Labor and quickly resorted to the strike weapon when union recognition and higher wage scales were denied them. From the enactment of the Recovery Act until its annual convention in October, 1933, the A. F. of L. reported the issuance of 700 charters to new federal unions, a great growth in membership in affiliated internationals, and the spread of unionization into industries like steel, automobiles, textiles, tires, oil, and aluminum, where earlier efforts at organization had always proved abortive. Before long the A. F. of L. was claiming a strength of 4,500,000 members, which was in excess of its previous highest development in 1920. In addition, independent unions not affiliated with the A. F. of L. and often having progressive leadership had a membership of at least 250,000 workers; while unions affiliated with the Communist Trade Union Unity League claimed 125,000 members.

Particularly significant was the growth of federal unions, organizations directly chartered by the A. F. of L., usually based on single shops and as a rule cutting across the craft lines of the old internationals. From July, 1933 to May, 1934, a total of 1,368 charters had been granted and some 800,000 workers had been unionized under them. In the automobile industry alone there were more than 150 of these federal unions. Into these new organizations were pouring young, enthusiastic, and militant workers who were unfamiliar and impatient with the conciliatory tactics of the older craft-union leadership and who refused to effect any agreements with their employers short of trade-union recognition. The fact of the matter was, many of the strikes following the inauguration of the NRA were rank-and-file struggles which were led not by the officers of the old unions but by strike committees made up directly of workers in the shops.

Confronted by such strength, it at once became apparent that the NRA was beginning to look on organized labor as something of a Frankenstein. It was all very well to permit the workers to combine so that through collective bargaining they might readjust any inequities that appeared as a result of rises in the cost of living; but did labor have to have outside leaders and could it not, as a patriotic act, surrender the use of the strike weapon and put its trust implicitly in the government?

A foreshadowing of the stand the National Recovery Administrator was to take was indicated in the letter of resignation of Dudley Cates, Assistant Administrator for Industry, on August 31, 1933. In this he insisted that the conventional types of trade unions (i. e., organizations formed by the workers themselves and directed by their own leaders) were "essentially provocative." Mr. Cates continued:

The underlying purpose of the NIRA is to create a balanced economy in the United States. The industry, therefore, should be the unit in establishing the field of collective bargaining. . . . This means a vertical union in each industry, free of domination or control, either by employers or outside labor leaders. . . .

General Johnson, speaking before the A. F. of L. convention on October 10, released a preliminary shaft. "Labor," he said, "does not need to strike under the Roosevelt plan." The General went on:

Thus from the beginning to the end of this process [code-making and the adjustment of labor disputes] you are given a complete and highly effective protection of your rights. The plain, stark truth is that you cannot tolerate the strike. . . . If now—when the whole power of this government and its people are being given to an effort to provide and maintain to the ultimate the rights of every man who works for pay—you permit or countenance this economic sabotage, that public confidence and opinion will turn against you. . . .

Finally on November 1, when he gave his approval to the Swope plan, General Johnson revealed it as his intention to abandon labor altogether. He said then flatly:

I think these industrial groups are set up in order to have peace and equity, and that the labor group should be set right up beside that of industry with the strike and lockout absolutely eliminated, and with arrangements for the settlement of all disputes. Under the present conditions if there is an abuse in a particular company against labor it may become widespread. But if they are organized under this plan they are partners. . . .

To many, this scheme strikingly resembled the characteristic set-up of the fascist labor organizations of Italy and Germany; it was no wonder, therefore, that General Johnson increasingly came to be regarded as a foe of the organized workers of the country.

Equally disappointing was the position adopted by the National Labor Board. The board, in its effort to avert and adjust industrial disputes, perfected a formula which consisted of the following parts: workers out on strike were to return to their shops; the employers, in their turn, were to rehire all the workers without discrimination; the board was then to supervise an election of employee representatives for the purpose of collective bargaining. The fatal flaw in the plan lay in the fact that it was based upon ready acceptance by the employer; if the employer questioned the right of the board to supervise elections its only recourse lay in resort to the cumbersome legal machinery of the courts. The fact is, while small employers accepted the jurisdiction of the board, larger ones resisted, with the result that workers came to look upon the agency as impotent in the face of the recalcitrance of the great industrialists.

Between the summer of 1933 and June 1, 1934, the National Labor Board and its 19 Regional Labor Boards, in the 3,755 disputes they handled and which involved some 2,000,000 workers, were able to send back to work 1,270,000. The boards mediated 1,323 strikes, of which three-fourths were settled, and it averted 497 other strikes. In spite of this apparently favorable showing Senator Wagner, chairman of the board, confessed that the record "has a disquieting aspect. Its percentage of settlement is too low and some of the settlements have been unsatisfactory." Indeed, in a number of outstanding disputes, the board had been openly defied and the right to the free election of workers' representatives, to which it was pledged, had been flouted. This had happened in the cases of the disputes involving the thousands of workers of the Harriman Hosiery Mills of Harriman, Tenn., the so-called captive coal mines of the United States Steel Corporation in western Pennsylvania, the E. G. Budd Manufacturing Co. of Philadelphia, the Carnegie Steel Co. of Duquesne, Pa., the automobile manufacturers of Detroit and elsewhere, and the Weirton Steel Co. of West Virginia. In the last named, after a strike had dragged on wearily for months, the National Labor Board had succeeded in bringing about a settlement on the basis of a free election of employee representatives. But when a member of the board appeared to supervise the election, he was defied by the company union (which was backed up by the Weirton Steel Co.). The board applied to the federal district court of Wilmington, Del. for an injunction to restrain the steel company from interfering with the free election. Much to the board's embarrassment—and the act tied its hands completely—in May, 1934, the federal court refused to enjoin the Weirton Steel Co. from interfering with the election of workers' spokesmen for the purpose of collective bargaining under the National Labor Board's supervision. The judge ruled that under the Norris-La Guardia Anti-Injunction Law of 1932 a federal court might not grant even the United States government itself an injunction "unless the testimony of witnesses is heard in open court, with opportunity for cross-examination." It was apparent that the Administration had been rendered powerless to carry out its promise to permit labor to organize for the purpose of collective bargaining.

It was not until March 2, 1934, that organized labor gained a clear-cut victory through a decision of the National Labor Board; and even this was short-lived. In the case of the Denver Tramway Co., where balloting had taken place for the choice of the workers' spokesmen and a majority had elected to be represented by the Amalgamated Association of Street and Electric Railway Employees (an A. F. of L. union), the board ruled that the vote was binding on all the workers and that the outside union was to be regarded as the sole collective bargaining agency here. It was true that the closed shop was not recognized but that this decision was a precedent of the first importance was generally acknowledged.

Nevertheless, in less than three weeks its significance was destroyed. The threat of a general strike in the automobile industry over the question of recognition, by the end of March, 1934, had become so real that Roosevelt himself was forced to intervene. On March 25 the President announced a settlement which called for

the following: the return of the men to work; the establishment
of an Automobile Labor Board, made up of a labor representative,
an industry representative, and a "neutral"; the recognition of the
organizations of the men, their representatives to be chosen, however, not on the basis of majority selection but on that of propor-
tional representation (which meant the continuance of the open
shop and the acceptance of company unions); and the rehiring of
workers discharged for union activities. This plan the President
characterized as "a new course in social engineering"; before a
month was over it was plain that it had failed. In the words of
Louis Stark: "The automobile agreement, which placed labor on
the defensive, has had a devastating effect on its status. It began
by shattering the morale of the National Labor Board and reducing its precedents to so much paper." Further, the new Automobile Labor Board displayed its ineffectualness by refusing to deal
with the only question that interested the workers, that of union
recognition, but spent all its time elaborately examining cases of
discrimination because of union affiliations. The workers quickly
showed their dissatisfaction and strikes broke out in automobile
plants in St. Louis, Cleveland, Flint, and Toledo.

These rebuffs to labor had a profoundly disillusioning effect.
The result was, by the midsummer of 1934, it was commonly
charged that section 7 (a) had been nullified, the President's automobile settlement had played into the hands of the industrialists
by underwriting company unionism, and that government agencies
were powerless to gain union recognition. Labor fell back on the
only economic weapon in its armory, the strike. The table on page
120 indicates the growing unrest of labor under the New Deal.
What was particularly significant about the disputes of the past
year, as compared with those of earlier years, was the fact that
in the great majority of cases walkouts and lockouts were due to
failure to obtain union recognition. Thus, as Herman Feldman has
pointed out, wage issues, either singly or combined with other issues, figured in three-fifths of all the strikes of the ten years
1916–26; during 1933–34, only one-fifth of the disputes involved
wages. In 1916–26, recognition of the union constituted barely
one-fifth of the total causes for industrial disputes; in 1933–34,
the proportion was at least three-fourths.

The wave of strikes that was sweeping the country in 1934 and
involving some of its greatest industries had these common char-

Year	Employees Directly Involved in Strikes	Man-Days Lost in Disputes *
1929	230,463	9,975,213
1930	158,114	2,730,368
1931	279,299	6,386,183
1932	242,826	6,462,973
1933	812,137	14,818,847
1933		
Jan.–Mar. inc.	70,438	796,543
Apr.–June	105,632	1,643,124
July–Sept.	489,056	6,448,813
Oct.–Dec.	122,131	4,567,278
1934		
Jan.–Mar. inc.	195,642	3,806,611
April & May	303,335	6,415,408

* Strikes and lockouts

acteristics: the leadership generally was from the rank and file; it accepted support of radical groups, including not only revolutionary organizations but those of unemployed councils and leagues; it refused the offers of arbitration of labor boards; it met violence with violence and to lockouts, injunctions, and the use of armed guards and militia, it replied with mass picketing, attacks on scabs, defiance of police and soldiers, and the destruction of plants and movable property; and as a *sine qua non* of industrial peace it demanded trade union recognition. During May, June, and July, 1934, major strikes were everywhere in effect, including the longshoremen and marine workers of the Pacific and Gulf ports, fruit and vegetable pickers of California, Ohio and New Jersey, iron ore and copper miners of the Far West, coal miners of the border states and the South, textile workers of Alabama, steel workers of the Middle West, automobile mechanics of the Lake states, electrical workers of Milwaukee, taxi drivers, shoe workers and meat workers of New York, and truckers of Minneapolis. From January to August, 1934, so bitterly fought were these disputes, twenty-eight workers were killed in strikes and other labor troubles.

Characteristic of the temper of labor was the open industrial warfare that broke out in Toledo in May, 1934. The Electric Auto-Lite Co., a member of the Automobile Chamber of Commerce and as such hostile to trade unionism, refused the demands of its workers for a wage increase and recognition of their A. F. of L. federal union, the United Automobile Workers' Federal Union, No. 18384. In February the workers in this plant and those of two affiliated companies struck and so aggressively did they carry on their strike activities that in March the company was forced to yield. A compromise was effected under which a partial wage increase was granted, shop committees were recognized, and the company promised to open negotiations for a union contract on April 1. When the company, on that date, rejected the request of the workers for the discussion of the question of the closed shop, the workers on April 12 went out once more and resumed picketing, this time enlisting the support of the Lucas County Unemployed League to prevent the recruitment of strike-breakers. The company's reply was the suing out of an injunction against the federal union and the unemployed league; this was immediately granted and the court enjoined the strikers and their sympathizers from engaging in mass picketing.

On May 7 the Lucas County Unemployed League announced that it would openly defy the injunction and begin mass picketing again; and despite the frequent arrests of the leaders mass picketing was resumed, on May 23 as many as 10,000 men and women collecting around the company gates. Meanwhile, the company had offered to pay the salaries of deputy sheriffs and the sheriff of the county deputized 150 guards to protect the property of the plant and break up the picket line. Sporadic fighting took place all day. When iron bolts were thrown out of the factory windows and tear gas was released from its roof, in the words of the *New Republic:* "The crowd quickly reacted. They hurled bricks and stones into the plant, cut off the light supply, rammed the doors of the plant with great timbers, and continued a battle with police and deputies all through the night. The strike-breakers meanwhile were imprisoned in the plant." The same night some 1,000 members of the National Guard appeared on the scene armed with tear and nausea gas equipment and firearms; these were used and in the street battles that followed the militia killed two persons and wounded scores, while the workers retaliated with bricks, bottles, and other crude missiles. The threats of a walk-out by the Toledo Edison workers, which would have paralyzed the industrial life of the whole city, and that of a general strike by the Central Labor

Union of Toledo and the A. F. of L. locals affiliated with it, forced the hand of the Electric Auto-Light Co. On June 5, an agreement was signed between the company and the federal union which recognized the union as the representative of the workers and promised no discrimination against workers for union activities, while guaranteeing seniority rights, the return of their jobs to all strikers, and a 5 per cent wage increase. This union contract was the first one to be drawn up in the automobile industry. It had been won, as Louis F. Budenz, the leader of the mass pickets described it, "through intelligent mass action, defiance of capitalist courts, vigorous class warfare."

Perhaps even more ominous, as far as continued industrial strife was concerned, was the possibility of a general steel strike, the first one in the industry since 1919, which threatened to involve some 400,000 workers. Dissatisfied with the repeated refusals of the steel companies to permit the workers to bargain collectively through representatives of their own choosing, the Amalgamated Association of Iron, Steel, and Tin Workers (an A. F. of L. union), through a rank-and-file committee, in June, 1934, called upon Secretary of Labor Perkins and National Recovery Administrator Johnson to obtain for them a conference with their employers for the purpose of discussing their grievances. At the same time, in a petition to the President, the committee charged that the iron and steel code had been extended beyond its preliminary period "without any material change in its labor provisions" and that the Administrator in recommending this extension had "neglected to hold a public hearing or to investigate labor practices, policies, or wages, hours of labor and conditions of employment in the steel industry."

The inability of Washington to obtain for the men the promise of a conference resulted in the meeting, at Pittsburgh on June 14, of a convention to discuss a strike. It was plain that the steel workers were in an impatient mood: the defeat of the government in the Weirton case, the refusal of their employers to treat with them, and the fear of another unsatisfactory settlement comparable to the automobile agreement were responsible for a remarkable unanimity of opinion; the rank and file would accept nothing less than an assurance of union recognition. It was only through the intervention of President William Green of the A. F. of L. that the general steel strike, scheduled to begin on June 16, was averted. Upon the advice of Green, the convention decided to submit the following compromise plan to President Roosevelt and the steel companies: the creation of an impartial board of three men to be appointed by the President; this board was to have authority to investigate and adjust complaints of violations of section 7 (a), to offer arbitration, and to hold independent elections of representatives of the men for the purpose of collective bargaining; the men selected by the majority of the workers were to be recognized by the steel companies as the spokesmen for all the workers; the board was to have access to company payrolls. In the event that affirmative action could not be secured on the Green proposal, the union's executive committee could go ahead with a strike call. The danger of a serious industrial dispute, of course, was not over; it had been postponed for a short time until Roosevelt could obtain the necessary concessions from the steel corporations.[2]

The Green proposal, in many particulars, was similar to the content of the Labor Disputes Joint Resolution passed by both houses of the Seventy-third Congress in one of the very last days of its regular session, June 16, 1934, and approved June 19; for this reason it was generally assumed that Green had gone to the Pittsburgh convention of the steel workers as an unofficial emissary from Washington. The Labor Disputes Resolution included the following six points: (1) The President was authorized to establish a board or boards empowered to investigate matters in disputes between workers and employers arising out of the NIRA; and upon the request of both parties to a dispute the board or boards were to act as agencies of voluntary arbitration. (2) Such agencies were to order and conduct elections among the workers in order to determine representation for the purpose of collective bargaining. The orders of these boards were to have the same status as those of the Federal Trade Commission and as such were enforceable by the federal courts. (It will be noted that nothing was said of majority rule in the case of workers' elections.) (3) The boards, with the approval of the President, were to prescribe such rules and regulations as might be necessary. (4) Persons who "knowingly" violated the edicts of the boards were to be punished by fine and imprisonment. (5) Boards established under the resolution were to cease to exist on June 16, 1935, the date of termination of the NIRA. (6) Nothing in the resolution was to prevent

---

[2] The National Steel Relations Labor Board, set up June 28, 1934, was given all these powers.

or diminish the right of workers to strike or engage in other concerted activities. It is significant to note that Congress rejected an
amendment that no board might establish or recognize a closed
shop.

This was a far cry from the original Wagner Labor Disputes
bill, which had been introduced in February, 1934, by the chairman of the National Labor Board in an effort to compel employer
observance of the labor provisions of the NIRA. The bill, as
drawn up in the beginning, had prohibited a number of "unfair
labor practices," among which the following were specifically
enumerated: the initiation and financing of company unions, interference with the selection of employee representatives, and refusal to recognize or deal with employee representatives. It had
also called for the creation of a permanent national labor board to
enforce its provisions, mediate labor disputes, and determine workers' representatives for purposes of collective bargaining. The
measure, due to the hostility of manufacturer groups, was pruned
and trimmed in committee with the result that its emasculated
form pleased neither its friends nor its foes. It was to create some
machinery for emergency use in industrial disputes that the President prevailed on Congressional leaders to substitute the Labor
Disputes Resolution for the Wagner bill; and in the very last days
of the session the resolution was jammed through, without even
a record vote in the House. On June 26, the President established
the National Longshoremen's Board, to investigate and arbitrate,
if called upon, the bitter strike involving thousands of waterfront
and marine workers in San Francisco; on June 28, the National
Steel Relations Labor Board was set up; and on July 9, the National Labor Board was abolished and in its place there was created
the National Labor Relations Board, of three members, independent of the NRA and working in conjunction with the Labor Department, which was to coördinate the various functions set out
in the Labor Disputes Resolution and act as a court of last review
for special labor boards. (In addition to those already cited there
were special boards in bituminous coal, cotton textiles, wool and
silk textiles, construction, etc.) It remained to be seen whether
any attempts at arbitration by federal agencies, which did not
among their powers have the right to order the recognition of
spokesmen of labor picked by majority vote, the establishment of
the closed shop, and whose decisions were devoid of punitive sanc-

tions, would be acceptable to workers who were beginning to feel that they had been led astray once too often by soft answers and fair promises.

A test appeared sooner than was anticipated; this was in the general strike which broke out in San Francisco and the Bay counties during July 16–19, 1934. The dispute had started as a conflict between the 12,000 local members of the International Longshoremen's Association (an A. F. of L. affiliate) and the San Francisco shipping interests, on May 9; within a week the longshoremen had enlisted the support of the 15,000 members of ten marine workers' unions in the area. Of those participating in the sympathetic strike, only one body was radical, the Marine Workers' Industrial Union; the others were A. F. of L. unions or independent unions having no revolutionary programs. The strike soon spread to the whole Pacific coast and completely crippled the operations of all ports. The demands of the workers centered in recognition of their unions, control by the men over the hiring halls (which, in effect, meant the closed shop), and improvement of working conditions.

The joint strike committee, which was led by Harry R. Bridges, was united on the following tactical principles: (1) the recognition of collective bargaining on industrial lines; (2) democratic control of the strike by the workers, so that all important questions could be submitted for referendum votes; (3) willingness to arbitrate every question in dispute except those of union recognition and union control of the hiring halls. In short, this was a rank-and-file revolt against the leadership of the conservative bureaucrats of the A. F. of L. unions. As John Powell, writing in the *New Republic* of August 8, 1934, put it: "At all three points it [the joint strike committee] ran head-on into the classic principles of the Federation, which is essentially a clearing-house of the log-rolling politics of separate craft unions, under the autocratic control of an oligarchy. . . ." The impatient attitude of the men toward the A. F. of L. leadership was plainly displayed by their reception of the "settlement" effected by the president of the International Longshoremen's Association, on June 16; this official's willingness to turn over the hiring halls of the longshoremen to an impartial committee and to desert the other marine workers was quickly repudiated and the strike went on. The workers were able to maintain their solidarity, gain new accretions (teamsters, for example, refused to haul cargoes from the docks), and reject offers of arbitration by the hastily created National Longshoremen's Board.

Early in July, having received the promise of assistance of the Industrial Association of San Francisco, an open-shop employers' group, the shipping companies decided to open up the port; and, convoyed by armed police, strike-breaking trucks began to move. Clashes broke out at once between police and strikers, there were disorders on July 3 and July 5, and on the latter day the police fired on pickets and bands of sympathizers. Two men were killed and thirty-two more were wounded, of whom two more died subsequently. The acting governor of California rushed national guards to the scene. Within the next week other labor groups joined the marine workers in sympathetic strikes; at the same time, public officials and the press particularly were becoming increasingly hostile. Talk of red control of the strike—which, never for a single instant, had existed—became very common.

On July 14, due to the constant pressure being exerted by the rank and file, the conservative Central Labor Council, which before had washed its hands of the strike, was compelled to move into action. Appreciating the importance of the principle of union recognition at stake, and seeking to channel the growing labor unrest into traditional grooves, the local A. F. of L. chiefs called a general strike for July 16. The order for the strike said nothing of political aims or the revolutionary overthrow of capitalism; indeed, so cautiously did the Central Labor Council move that its strike call rested labor's case entirely on the fact that employers were refusing to accord to workers the rights guaranteed them under the NIRA. In response, 75,000 workers in San Francisco and the East Bay and Upper East Bay communities at once downed tools and not a vehicle of transportation (except delivery wagons carrying milk and bread) moved, not a filling station, shop, or theater was open; but no essential services—water, power, light—were shut off. San Francisco walked and went without lunch; otherwise, there were no real discomforts and no disorders. Nonparticipants in the strike, generally, stood on the sidelines to watch the outcome of this trial of strength between capital and labor.

On the next day, however, the forces were mobilized for the breaking of the strike. A red hunt, egged on by the newspapers and led by vigilantes hired by the employers, with the police trailing behind not to arrest the attackers but the attacked, began; Communist and I. W. W. offices were forced open and wrecked; documents and files were confiscated; homes were broken into; men and women were cruelly beaten; and some three hundred persons were arrested, charged with vagrancy, and held under excessively high bail. Federal officials, instead of checking it, seemed to be willing to encourage the wave of terrorism. Secretary of Labor Perkins wired to Governor Merriam, promising federal support in the rounding up and deportation of radical aliens. General Johnson, who was on the coast as the unofficial representative of the Administration, openly indulged in a provocative act. Appearing at Berkeley, the seat of the University of California, to deliver a Phi Beta Kappa oration, the NRA head seized the opportunity to cheer on the forces of disorder. The strike he characterized as "civil war," "bloody insurrection," and "a blow at the flag of our common country"; if the federal government did not act, said the Administrator ominously, "the people would act, and it would act to wipe out this subversive element as you clean off a chalk mark on a blackboard with a wet sponge." And the general called upon "responsible labor organizations . . . to run these subversive elements out from its ranks like rats."

President William Green of the A. F. of L. the next day responded by disavowing the strike. The strike in San Francisco, he said, "is local in character, possessing no national significance"; and "the American Federation of Labor neither ordered the strike nor authorized it." Under such pressure the bewildered trade unionists, who had assumed that they were acting to defend their charter of liberties guaranteed by section 7(a) of the NIRA and who had not the slightest intention of effecting any political purpose through the general strike, began to drift back to work. On July 19, by a vote of 191 to 174 the general strike committee of the Central Labor Council decided to call the strike off; by a vote of 207 to 180 it agreed to submit the questions at issue to arbitration by the National Longshoremen's Board. At the end of four days the general strike was over. On July 24, the longshoremen voted to accept arbitration and on July 31 they returned to work. A concession gained was that men were to get back their jobs without discrimination either for union affiliation or strike activity; also, pending arbitration of the question, the men and the board were to have observers in the hiring halls; but provision was not made for the discharge of strike-breakers. The striking seamen were called upon to elect representatives for collective bargaining and arbitration and one group, the Sailors' Union of the Pacific, was recognized by the employers. Only time would tell whether the National Longshoremen's Board would be able to extract from the shipping interests, now that the West coast had become convinced that the strike was a revolutionary one, recognition of the unions of the marine workers.

Despite the nature of its ending, the strike was one of the greatest significance in American labor annals: it displayed the solidarity of the rank and file and its willingness to engage in struggle for a common purpose; and it showed that conservative trade union leaders were more interested in maintaining control over their unions than in antagonizing business and the press by engaging in sympathetic strikes. Finally, the issue of whether or not government agencies were going to demand employer recognition of the unions of the workers had been squarely joined.

The only definite step taken in the interest of labor was the passage of the Railway Pension bill (approved June 27) and the Crosser-Dill bill which revised the Railway Labor Act of 1926 (approved June 27). The first provided for a comprehensive retirement system for railway employees based on employer and employee contributions; the funds were to be held by the government and a Railroad Retirement Board was set up as the administrative agency. The second provided for the settlement of labor disputes affecting workers on the railways and in express and sleeping-car companies. Disputes were to be adjusted through collective bargaining, company unions were specifically outlawed, and bi-partisan adjustment boards were set up for arbitration purposes.

What Next?

To what point, after fifteen months of experimentation, had the New Deal brought the United States? The results, in general terms, can be summarized quickly. Farmers were getting higher prices but the spread between prices paid and prices received, which had been closed a little, was again widening. The total payroll of labor was increasing but retail prices were mounting faster, with the result that a decline in real wages, or purchasing power, had soon set in. Industrial recovery had reached a fairly high point by the summer of 1933; but it had dropped back in the winter and had then been followed by another upswing on a lower level, which already showed definite signs of receding in June, 1934. The capital goods industries continued to remain stagnant. Unemployment had scarcely been touched; relief expenditures steadily climbed higher. Only the very sanguine could claim that the New Deal had realized the expectations of its sponsors.

The just price, the principle upon which the New Deal was based, had not worked; the industrial, agricultural, and laboring classes would not, could not, stay in equilibrium. Indeed, certain institutional changes had been effected which indicated that class hostilities were already becoming more pronounced than ever before in recent American history. Both industry and labor had been organized: industry into cartels and labor into trade unions. Industry was already seeking to be free from government interference in order to push the processes of monopoly to their logical conclusion through the elimination of the small enterprisers, the maintenance of a monopoly price, and a constant pressure on its labor force. Labor, on the other hand—for the time being at any rate—had refused to surrender its independence: it stubbornly clung to the rights of organization under its own leaders, of union for common action, and of the use of the strike weapon. Whether the heads of the conservative unions would, however, yield to the blandishments of a Swope scheme and the patriotic exhortations of the President and the NRA and for promised security give up their freedom, it was for the time being impossible to say. Labor's leaders were, here and there, revealing a characteristic uncertainty; but the rank and file—as had happened so many times before in American industrial relations—was beginning to feel its strength it defied labor injunctions, it met official terrorism with positive evidences of working-class solidarity, and it was distrustful of all offers of arbitration. The mass of American workers was on the move; how far to the left it would go nobody yet knew and it was idle to hazard a prediction. But that the American worker was increasingly becoming class conscious none but the wilfully blind could deny.

The New Deal thus had turned out to be no revolution because it had effected no enduring changes in the class relations in American economic society. It had started out hopefully by attempting to allay class hostilities; it ended, ironically enough, by making the cleavage between classes more pronounced than it had ever been before. Agriculture was in a state of unrest. An organized capital and an organized labor confronted each other, like two hostile armies, across the narrow no-man's land of governmental regulation.

Would President Roosevelt sooner or later yield to the clamor of the inflationists? Despite the devaluation of the dollar, the passage of silver legislation, and the enactment of great emergency appropriation measures, it was plain that the soft money advocates had not been satisfied. With recovery sluggish, unemployment still great, and the burdens of debtors oppressive, attempts might yet be made to force inflation upon the country: perhaps by printing greenbacks to pay off a soldier bonus, or to retire maturing federal bonds and notes, or to launch more public works projects, or to finance the social services and relief activities of local jurisdictions verging on bankruptcy. Resort to the printing presses was an easy way of escaping daily difficulties; its cumulative and finally disastrous effects were best not thought of.

Looking a little farther into the future, would the United States try fascism, with the crushing of labor organizations and the frank utilization of the political state to preserve the position of capitalism and to depress the lot of the workers and farmers to meaner and meaner subsistence levels? Were the savage forays of vigilante groups in San Francisco and elsewhere auguries of what was to come soon on an organized scale? Or should we seek our salvation in a reversion to imperialist oversea expansion: not, of course, to old-fashioned territorial aggression but to struggles with rival powers for foreign markets—even at the risk of war?

Of these less immediate prospects fascism seemed more remote, another fling at financial and industrial imperialism the more likely probability. Fascism, as has been pointed out, was a counter-revolutionary device employed by capitalism only as a last desperate expedient. It seized the state, put an end to democracy and representative government, and ruthlessly crushed the opposition of militantly organized working-class groups for the purpose of continuing the economic processes of society solely in the interests of the owners of the means of production. But fascism needed a population that could be drilled into accepting a passionately avowed nationalist ideology; it required the support of a private army made up of permanently declassed members of the petty bourgeoisie; and none of these objective conditions could be said truthfully to exist in the United States.

Imperialism, on the other hand, was exactly cut to the measure of American capitalism in its present stage. Confronted by over-expansion of plant, possessing great capital reserves for which domestic investment opportunities continued to dwindle, mobilized —thanks to the NRA—into powerful cartels which could be immediately utilized as the spearheads in a drive for oversea markets, American capitalism was equipped and ready for imperialist adventure. Its inauguration waited on the approval of Washington. The United States could still make the Far Eastern and Latin-American markets exclusive financial and commercial American preserves. To build railroads and public utility systems, bridges, docks, assembling and distributing plants; to establish banks, foreign sales agencies, shipping companies: in short, to put to work once more our own capital goods industries, find outlets for our capital reserves, create foreign positions for professional and white-collar workers, and furnish employment at home for labor so that compliance would again be its distinguishing characteristic: was there a surer or easier road to recovery? Of course our attempt to possess the Chinese market would be contested by Japan, already, as we have seen, aware of that danger; our effort to monopolize Latin-American trade and financing would be challenged by Great Britain. But American resources, organization, and technical skill were so overwhelmingly superior to those of rival imperialist powers that Japanese and British competition could check our progress only slightly.

Surely, at the end of the imperialist road stood war? However, war entered into almost any calculation for the future. What lay in store for the United States in the next few years: A resurgent imperialism? Fascism? Proletarian revolution? It was not beyond the range of probability that the New Deal, before it had run its course, might yet be called upon to face one or another of these tests of fire.

APPENDIX I

LEGISLATIVE RECORD OF THE SEVENTY-THIRD CONGRESS

The Seventy-third Congress was called for its first session March 9, 1933 and sat until June 16, 1933. As a result of the ratification of the Twentieth Amendment, the second session did not convene until January 3, 1934. It sat until June 18, 1934. In this period the legislation of the New Deal was enacted; and the following presents the legislative record of this historic Congress. Where the laws have not been described in the text the comments below are somewhat fuller. These notes, in the main, are based on the excellent summary published in the New York *Times* of June 17, 1934.

AGRICULTURE

Agricultural Adjustment Act (approved May 12, 1933). Set up the Agricultural Adjustment Administration; provided for the establishment of parity prices for farm products and for the licensing and taxing of processors; provided for the refinancing of farm mortgages. Also included an inflationary program.

Farm Credit Act of 1933 (approved June 16, 1933). Authorized the Farm Credit Administration to centralize all agricultural credit activities.

Farm Mortgage Refinancing Act (approved January 31, 1934). Created the Federal Farm Mortgage Corporation to aid further in the refinancing of farm debts and guaranteed both as to principal and interest federal bonds exchanged for consolidated farm loan bonds.

Farm Mortgage Foreclosure Act (approved June 12, 1934). Extended the lending authority of the Land Bank Commissioner to permit him to make loans to farmers for the purpose of enabling them to redeem farm properties owned by them previous to foreclosure regardless of when such foreclosure took place.

Frazier-Lemke Farm Bankruptcy Act (approved June 28, 1934). Facilitated agreements between distressed farmers and their creditors and granted extensions of time to farmers during which they might remain in possession of their farms.

Crop Loan Act (approved February 23, 1934). Permitted the Farm Credit Administration to make loans to farmers in 1934 for crop production and harvesting.

Jones-Connally Farm Relief Act (approved April 7, 1934). Included among the basic crops of the original Agricultural Adjustment Act beef and dairy cattle, peanuts, rye, barley, flax, and grain sorghums; also provided funds for the control of diseased cattle.

Cotton Control Act (approved April 21, 1934). Placed the production of cotton on a compulsory instead of a voluntary basis.

Jones-Costigan Sugar Act (approved May 9, 1934). Included among the basic crops of the original Agricultural Adjustment Act sugar beets and sugar cane; fixed the domestic production of each commodity and authorized the Secretary of Agriculture to put all sugar imports on a quota basis.

Grazing Act (approved June 28, 1934). Provided for federal regulation of grazing on the public domain; authorized the Secretary of Interior to provide for the protection, orderly use, and regulation of public ranges and to create grazing districts with an aggregate area of not more than 80,000,000 acres.

Tobacco Control Act (approved June 28, 1934). Placed the production of tobacco on a compulsory basis.

AIR MAIL

Emergency Air Mail Act (approved March 27, 1934). Empowered the Postmaster General to conduct the air mail service directly with planes and other equipment received from the War Department.

Air Mail Act of 1934 (approved June 12, 1934). Authorized the Postmaster General to award new one-year contracts for air mail transportation to the lowest responsible bidders; reduced air mail postage rates to 6 cents an ounce; set up a commission to make a survey of air mail conditions; declared that the basic rate of pay to air mail carriers was not to exceed 33⅓ cents an airplane mile for transporting a mail load not exceeding 300 pounds and that the pay was not to exceed 40 cents for heavier loads; prevented the award of contracts to companies serving more than 29,000 miles of route; gave the Interstate Commerce Commission control over air mail rates; outlawed holding companies and interlocking directorates and limited salaries of officers and directors of air mail companies; gave the Secretary of Commerce control over maximum and minimum flying hours and other aspects of operation and carriage.

BANKING

Emergency Banking Relief Act (approved March 9, 1933). Gave President powers to regulate transactions in credit, currency, gold and silver, and foreign exchange; empowered Secretary of Treasury to require the delivery of all gold and gold certificates; provided for the appointment of conservators of national banks in difficulties; extended operations of Federal Reserve system.

Banking Act of 1933 (approved June 16, 1933). Extended Federal Reserve open market activities; created the Federal Bank Deposit Insurance Corporation to insure deposits; regulated further the operations of member banks; separated security affiliates; permitted branch banking.

Bank Deposit Insurance Act (approved June 19, 1934). Amended deposit features of Banking Act and raised amount eligible for insurance of each depositor to $5,000; postponed termination of insurance of non-member banks until July 1, 1937.

State Bank Aid Act (approved March 24, 1934). Permitted state banks and trust companies not members of the Federal Reserve system for one year to borrow directly from Federal Reserve Banks the same as member banks.

Collateral Security Act (approved March 9, 1934). Extended until March 3, 1935, the time in which the Federal Reserve Banks may be permitted to use United States bonds as security for the issuance of their notes and credits.

BANKRUPTCY

Municipal Bankruptcy Act (approved May 24, 1934). For two years cities and other local taxing units might petition the federal courts to approve plans for the readjustment of their debts if holders of 51 per cent of outstanding obligations consented; the plan of readjustment was not to be authorized by the court until approved by creditors holding two-thirds of each class of claims affected and of those holding three-fourths of the amount of all securities.

Corporate Bankruptcy Act (approved June 7, 1934). Permitted corporations to reorganize with the consent of the majority of their creditors and allowed financial compromises where a majority of creditors had agreed; declared that a petition for reorganization might be filed by a creditor or stockholder if approved by holders of 25 per cent in amount of any class of creditors; that when corporations were not insolvent but were unable to meet maturing obligations, agreement to the petition was to come from stockholders representing 10 per cent of any class of stock; provided for the guidance of the federal courts.

COMMUNICATIONS

Communications Act of 1934 (approved June 19, 1934). Created a federal commission to regulate interstate and foreign communications services by telegraph, telephone, cable, and radio; abolished the Federal Radio Commission and transferred its functions as well as those of the Interstate Commerce Commission as regards telephone and telegraph to the new commission; repealed the Radio Act of 1927 and made new regulations for the control of radio broadcasting.

CRIME

Six Federal Crime Control Acts (approved May 18, 1934). Provided for the punishment for killing, assaulting, resisting, opposing, impeding, or interfering with federal officers while performing their duties in coping with crime; applied the powers of the federal government, under the commerce clause of the Constitution, to extortion by means of telephone, telegraph, radio, and oral message; provided punishment by death, if jury so recommends, for the transportation of kidnapped persons in interstate commerce; made it unlawful for any person to flee from one state to another in order to avoid prosecution or giving testimony in cases involving murder, kidnapping, burglary, robbery, mayhem, or extortion accompanied by acts of violence; provided punishment of 10 years imprisonment for causing or assisting in prison mutiny, riot, or escape; provided punishment for certain offenses committed against banks organized or operated under laws of the United States or any member-bank of the Federal Reserve system.

Crime Prevention Compact Act (approved June 16, 1934). Gave Congress's consent to compacts by states for coöperative effort to prevent crime and the enforcement of their respective criminal laws and policies; permitted the creation of joint state agencies for this purpose.

Arrest Facilitation Act (approved June 6, 1934). Appropriated for reward purposes sums of money to facilitate the arrest of persons charged with violation of the criminal laws of the United States or any state.

National Stolen Property Act (approved May 22, 1934). Extended the provisions of the National Motor Vehicle Theft Act of 1919 to other stolen property transported in interstate commerce.

EMPLOYMENT

National Employment System Act (approved June 6, 1933). Set up a national employment system and provided for coöperation with similar state agencies; provided for matching federal appropriations to states maintaining employment services.

Roads Employment Act (approved June 18, 1934). Authorized appropriations for emergency construction of public highways without matching by states during 1935 and 1936, as an employment measure.

HOME FINANCING

Home Owners' Refinancing Act (approved June 13, 1933). Created the Home Owners' Loan Corporation to refinance home mortgages.

Home Owners' Loan Act of 1934 (approved April 27, 1934). Guaranteed the principal of the HOLC's bond issues; and permitted loans for repairs of dwellings.

National Housing Act (approved June 28, 1934). Created a thorough-going scheme of home financing and mortgage insurance and offered protection to financial institutions making loans for financing repairs, alterations, and improvements; set up the Federal Housing Administration; increased the borrowing power of the HOLC to $3,000,000,000.

INSURANCE

Insurance Company Loan Act (approved June 10, 1933). Authorized RFC to subscribe to insurance company preferred stock and to make loans upon such stock; empowered the RFC to make loans to state workmen's compensation funds.

LABOR

Kick-Back Racket Act (approved June 13, 1933). Unlawful for contractors at work on public works to demand that workers give back part of their wages.

Labor Disputes Joint Resolution (approved June 19, 1934). Abolished the National Labor Board and created a federal agency for the investigation and mediation of labor disputes arising out of the NIRA.

Railway Pension Act (approved June 27, 1934). Provided a comprehensive retirement system for railway employees based on employer and employee contributions.

Crosser-Dill Railway Labor Act (approved June 27, 1934). Provided for the settlement of labor disputes on the railroads; company unions were specifically outlawed.

LIQUOR

Beer-Wine Revenue Act (approved March 22, 1933). Levied a tax of $5 on every barrel of beer and wine manufactured; reënacted portions of the Webb-Kenyon Act as a protection to states whose laws prohibited liquors of more alcoholic content than 3.2 per cent by weight; left to states all regulatory and control measures, particularly the method of distribution.

Liquor-Taxing Act of 1934 (approved January 11, 1934). Imposed taxes on distilled spirits, beer, and wines; amended the Reed law of 1917 to permit publications carrying liquor advertisements to circulate in dry states.

MONEY

Gold Repeal Joint Resolution (approved June 5, 1933). Canceled the gold clause in all federal and private obligations and made them payable in legal tender.

Gold Reserve Act of 1934 (approved January 30, 1934). Authorized the President to revalue the dollar at 50 to 60 cents in terms of its gold content; set up a $2,000,000,000 stabilization fund.

Silver Purchase Act (approved June 19, 1934). Authorized the President to nationalize silver.

MUNITIONS

Arms Sale Resolution (approved May 28, 1934). If the President issued a proclamation forbidding the sale of munitions to the countries engaged in the Chaco dispute, such sales were to be unlawful.

NATIONAL DEFENSE

National Guard Act of 1934 (approved June 15, 1934). Made the National Guard a part of the army of the United States in time of war or when Congress declared a national emergency to exist.

Vinson Naval Parity Act (approved March 27, 1934). Approved building the navy up to the treaty limits authorized by the Washington Treaty of 1922 and the London Treaty of 1930.

NATIONALITY

Equal Nationality Act (approved May 24, 1934). Amended the Cable Act of 1922 so as to remove all discrimination against women in the nationality laws.

RAILROADS

Emergency Railroad Transportation Act of 1933 (approved June 16, 1933). Set up a federal Coördinator of Transportation.

RECOVERY

National Industrial Recovery Act (approved June 16, 1933). Provided for the establishment of a National Recovery Administration to supervise the preparation of codes of fair competition and to guarantee labor's rights to organize and bargain collectively; provided for a program of public works; provided for petroleum control and for expenditures for state highways and subsistence homesteads.

Loans-to-Industry Act (approved June 19, 1934). Authorized direct loans to industry, not to exceed $500,000 to any one organization; empowered the RFC to furnish $75,000,000 for school districts to pay teachers' delinquent salaries and $25,000,000 to drainage districts.

RELIEF

Wagner-Lewis $500,000,000 Emergency Relief Act (approved May 12, 1933). Authorized the RFC to make $500,000,000 available for emergency relief purposes to be spent by the FERA created by the act.

CCC Reforestation Relief Act (approved March 31, 1933). Authorized the President to provide work for unemployed American citizens in reforestation and the like, and to establish camps for their housing, and to furnish them with cash allowances.

Civil Works-Emergency Relief Act (approved February 15, 1934). Appropriated an additional $950,000,000, available until June 30, 1935, for continuation of the civil works program and for direct relief purposes under authority of the FERA.

RFC Extension Act (approved January 20, 1934). Provided for the continuance of the functions of the RFC as a lending body until February 1, 1935, after which it would become only a liquidating corporation.

RFC Exports Resolution (approved March 26, 1934). Declared that in any loans made by the RFC or other federal instrumentality to foster exports of agricultural or other products provision should be made that such products should be carried exclusively in vessels of the United States.

SECURITIES

Securities Act of 1933 (approved May 27, 1933). Provided for filing with the Federal Trade Commission and for transmission to prospective investors fullest possible information, accompanied by sworn statements, about new security issues sold in interstate commerce or through the mails.

Securities Exchange Act (approved June 6, 1934). Provided for the regulation of securities exchanges and established a Securities and Exchange Commission.

TARIFF

Reciprocal Tariff Act (approved June 12, 1934). Authorized the President, for a period of three years, to negotiate trade agreements with foreign governments without the advice and consent of the Senate; gave the President the power to raise and lower tariff rates by not more than 50 per cent.

TAXATION

Gasoline Tax and Postage Rate Act (approved June 16, 1933). Continued the federal 1 cent-a-gallon gasoline tax until June 30, 1934;

authorized the President to proclaim modifications of postal rates on mail matter; imposed a 3 per cent tax on the price of electrical energy sold for domestic or commercial consumption.

Revenue Act of 1934 (approved May 10, 1934). Removed part of the burden on small income taxpayers in the "earned income" class and shifted it more to those whose incomes came from "unearned sources"; repealed the bank check tax as of January 1, 1935; provided for publicity on certain facts relating to each income return, including the amount of gross income and credits against net income and the total tax paid; imposed a processing tax of 3 cents a pound on a list of vegetable and fish oils and fats, and a tax of 5 cents a pound on cocoanut oil and copra except on imports from the Philippines, which products would bear the 3 cents tax.

VETERANS

Economy Act of 1933 (approved March 20, 1933). Repealed existing laws relating to benefits for World War and Spanish War veterans and authorized the President to establish a new pension system.

Independent Offices Appropriations Act (passed over Presidential veto March 28, 1934). Provided more liberal benefits for veterans, particularly as regards veterans having presumptive disabilities.

VOCATIONAL AID

Vocational Education Act of 1934 (approved May 21, 1934). Provided for the further development of vocational education as an emergency measure during the depression by appropriating $3,000,000 annually for three years.

WATER POWER

Tennessee Valley Authority Act (approved May 18, 1933). Created the Tennessee Valley Authority to maintain and operate Muscle Shoals and to develop the water power resources of the Tennessee Valley region and raise the economic and social level of the valley.

Electric Rate Investigation Resolution (approved April 14, 1934). Ordered the Federal Power Commission to investigate and compile the rates charged for electric energy by private and municipal corporations and to report to Congress.

FOREIGN AFFAIRS AND DEPENDENCIES

Johnson Debt Default Act (approved April 13, 1934). Prohibited financial transactions with foreign governments in default in the payment of their obligations, or any part thereof, to the government of the United States.

Free Trade Zone Act (approved June 18, 1934). Provided for the establishment, operation, and maintenance of foreign-trade zones in ports of entry of the United States; into these foreign commodities might be imported free of duties for manufacture and ultimate sale abroad.

Equal Rights Nationality Treaty (ratified May 24, 1934). Adopted at the Pan-American Conference at Montevideo on December 26, 1933, it provided that there should be no distinction based on sex as regards nationality, in the legislation and practice of the twenty countries in the Western Hemisphere participating.

Cuban Treaty (ratified May 31, 1934). Abrogated the Platt Amendment which permitted the United States to intervene in Cuba.

Trade in Arms Treaty (ratified June 15, 1934). Signed at Geneva on June 17, 1925; provided for the supervision of the international trade in arms and ammunition.

Anti-War Treaty of Non-Aggression (ratified June 15, 1934). Signed at Rio de Janeiro, October 10, 1934, by a group of Western Hemisphere countries; condemned war and advocated the settlement of disputes through the pacific means established by international law; declared that territorial questions must not be settled by resort to violence and that parties to the treaty would recognize no territorial arrangement not obtained through pacific means.

Convention on Rights and Duties of States (ratified June 15, 1934). Signed at Montevideo on December 26, 1933, by countries participating in the Pan-American Conference; defined the rights and duties of States and provided that no State had the right to intervene in the internal or external affairs of another.

Tydings-McDuffie Philippine Independence Act (approved March 24, 1934). Provided for independence of the Philippines following the expiration of ten years from the inauguration of the new Philippine government provided for in the act.

APPENDIX II

THE COURSE OF RECOVERY IN INDEX NUMBERS

(1923–25, monthly average = 100, unless otherwise indicated)

	March, 1933	July, 1933	December, 1933	January, 1934	February, 1934	March, 1934	April, 1934	May, 1934
1aIndustrial production	59	100	75	78	81	85	81	87
1aConstruction contracts awarded	14	21	58	49	44	33	32	26
1bFactory employment	59	73	75	75	78	81	82	82
2bFactory payrolls	37	51	55	54	61	65	67	61
1aFreight-car loadings	50	65	62	64	64	66	62	64
1cDepartment store sales	57	70	69	69	71	77	77	77
1cDepartment store stocks	54	60	65	66	66	65	65	66
2cStocks of manufactured goods	97	104	110	111	111	108	109	108
3bWholesale prices	60	69	71	72	74	74	73	74
4dCost of Living	72	75	77	78	78	79	78	79
5bRetail prices—food	91	105	104	105	108	109	107	108
7fFarm prices	50	76	68	70	76	76	74	74
7fPrices paid by farmers	100	107	116	117	119	120	120	121
7fRatio of prices rec'd by farmers to prices paid	50	71	59	60	64	63	62	61
1cForeign trade, value–exports	28	43	48	44	47	50	50	45
1cForeign trade, value—imports	26	48	42	42	42	44	42	47
6eBank debits outside New York City	9,608	13,878	13,288	13,198	11,784	14,077	14,278	14,105
6eLoans on securities *	3,644	3,772	3,620	3,609	3,520	3,514	3,577	3,476
6eAll other loans *	4,688	4,774	4,765	4,740	4,665	4,647	4,559	4,550
6eInvestments *	7,669	8,011	8,200	8,772	9,215	9,311	9,326	9,280

1 Adjusted for seasonal variation
2 Unadjusted
3 Monthly average, 1926 = 100
4 Monthly average, 1923 = 100
5 Monthly average, 1913 = 100
6 In millions of dollars, averages of daily figures
7 August, 1909–July, 1914 = 100

a Federal Reserve Board
b Bureau of Labor Statistics
c Bureau of Foreign and Domestic Commerce
d National Industrial Conference Board
e Federal Reserve Board
f Bureau of Agricultural Economics
* Reporting member banks

143

BIBLIOGRAPHY

GENERAL BACKGROUND. An excellent discussion of the economic and social conditions of the country immediately preceding the inauguration of the New Deal is to be found in Mauritz A. Hallgren, *Seeds of Revolt* (1933). Books setting forth the problems and techniques of social planning are George Soule, *A Planned Society* (1932) and Stuart Chase, *A New Deal* (1932). Lewis Corey, *The Decline of American Capitalism* (1934), a radical analysis of the economics of capitalism before the New Deal, is one of the most significant books to have appeared in the United States in the postwar period. An excellent critique of the New Deal, in terms of the fundamental economic and class problems it has tried to cope with, is to be found in George Soule, *The Coming American Revolution* (1934). A. A. Berle, Jr. and G. C. Means, *The Modern Corporation and Private Property* and H. W. Laidler, *Concentration in American Industry* (1931) treat of the development of monopoly capitalism. Evans Clark and others, *The Internal Debts of the United States* (1933) is highly useful. Stuart Chase, *The Economy of Abundance* (1934) is a popular presentation of some of the perplexities of modern-day America. R. G. Tugwell, *Industrial Discipline and the Governmental Arts* (1933) presents the rationale of the New Deal by one of its leading theoreticians. F. D. Roosevelt, *Looking Forward* (1933) is largely made up of the President's campaign addresses; *On Our Way* (1934) is a collection of Presidential speeches and State papers. A. N. Holcombe, *The New Party Politics* (1934) discusses the politics of planning and the New Deal.

GENERAL TREATMENTS. E. K. Lindley, *The Roosevelt Revolution: First Phase* (1933) was the first and in many ways is still the best general discussion of the inauguration of the New Deal. Charles A. Beard, *The Future Comes* (1933) is a friendly analysis. Other discussions, for the most part hostile and representing the neo-classical positions in economics, are: D. V. Brown and others, *The Economics of the Recovery Program* (1933); L. P. Ayres, *Economics of Recovery* (1933); William MacDonald, *The Menace of Recovery* (1934); Columbia University Commission, *Economic Reconstruction* (1934). Walter Lippmann, *The Method of Freedom* is the work of a conservative publicist. A. A. Berle, Jr. and others, *America's Recovery Program* (1934) is a series of lectures by a group of New Deal theoreticians. Norman Thomas, *The Choice Before Us* (1934) is a socialist view. Bernard Faÿ, *Roosevelt and His America* (1933) is the enthusiastic report of a Frenchman. John Strachey, *The Coming Struggle for Power* (revised edition, 1934) has an excellent critical chapter on the New Deal by this radical publicist. W. F. Ogburn, editor, *Social Change and the New Deal* (1934) is an interesting symposium. James D. Magee and others, *The National Recovery Program* (1933) is a convenient summary. Anonymous, *The New Dealers*

145

(1934) is the best of the informal books about the men making the New Deal. S. C. Wallace's series of weekly articles in *Today* under the caption "Today's Lessons in Government" (begun November 4, 1933) should be read for an excellent running commentary on the theoretical and administrative aspects of the New Deal. The National Emergency Council (a government agency) publishes a loose-leaf manual called *Emergency Recovery Agencies and Facilities*.

SPECIAL TREATMENTS. The following titles suggest the subject matter discussed: C. L. Dearing and others, *The ABC of the NRA* (1934); B. S. Kirsh and H. R. Shapiro, *The National Industrial Recovery Act* (1933); L. Valenstein and E. B. Weiss, *Business Under the Recovery Act* (1933); George Terborgh, *Price Control Devices in NRA Codes* (1934); Emanuel Stein and others, *Labor and the New Deal* (1934); C. R. Daugherty, *Labor Under the NRA* (1934); O. Tead and H. C. Metcalf, *Labor Relations Under the Recovery Act* (1933); Louis Adamic, *Dynamite* (revised edition, 1934) has an excellent chapter on labor under the NRA; Wilson Gee, *American Farm Policy* (1934); H. A. Wallace, "America Must Choose" (1934), the statement for the revival of foreign trade by the Secretary of Agriculture; M. Ezekiel and L. H. Bean, "Economic Bases of the Agricultural Adjustment Act" (1933), the work of the economic advisers of the Secretary of Agriculture and the Agricultural Adjustment Administration.

INDEX

Acreage reduction, voluntary, 34; failure of in cotton, 93; in tobacco, 96 f.

Agricultural Adjustment Act, sent to Congress, 29; passed, 33 f., 133; acreage reduction, voluntary, 34; marketing agreements, 38; and increase of the amount of money in circulation, 54; surplus agricultural products and Federal Surplus Relief Corporation, 71.

Agriculture, depression in, reasons and background, 29 ff.; New Dealers' theory of recovery in, 29 ff.; changed international position of, 32; reasons for growing efficiency of, 33; failure of voluntary acreage reduction in, 93 ff.; threat to efficiency of as a result of production control, 96 f.; impossibility of revival of markets, 97 f.; and subsistence homesteads, 100 ff.; chances of saving it, 106 f.; after fifteen months, 128.

Air Mail Act of 1934, 134.

"America Must Choose," pamphlet by Secretary Wallace, 73, 96.

American Federation of Labor, report on wage increase, 86; increased membership of, 115; in election in Denver Tramway Company, 118; in Toledo strike, 121 f.; in San Francisco general strike, 125 ff.

Anti-War Treaty of Non-Aggression, 141.

Arms Sale Resolution, 138.

Arrest Facilitation Act, 136.

Baker, O. E., 32 f.

Bank Deposit Insurance Act, 135.

Bankhead Cotton Control Act, 96, 134.

Banking Act of 1933. *See* Glass-Steagall Act.

Banks, closing, 19 f.; Emergency Banking Act, 20, 134; Glass-Steagall Act, 63, 135.

Beer and wine, legislation, 22.

Beer-Wine Revenue Act, 137.

Blue Eagle, 46.

Brain Trust, in campaign, 16; in early planning of New Deal, 20.

Budget, federal, during New Deal, 81 ff.

Cabinet appointments, 20.

China, American and Japanese interest in, 78 ff.

Civil Works Administration, money allotment by PWA, 52; established, 70.

Civil Works Emergency Relief Act, 139.

Civilian Conservation Corps, established, 22, 139; money allotment by PWA, 52.

Code Authority, agency of self-government in industry, 46 ff.

Code-making, drawing up codes, 45; signing, 47; in cotton textile, 47; features of, 48.

Codes of fair competition, 41.

Collateral Security Act, 135.

Communications Act of 1934, 135.

Compliance Board, in charge of enforcement of NRA codes, 43, 45 f.

Consumers' Advisory Board, established, 43; quoted, 111.

Convention on Rights and Duties of States, 141.

Corn-hog program, 38.

Corporate Bankruptcy Act, 135.

Cotton, AAA's program for reduction in, 34 f.; Bankhead Cotton Control Act, 95, 134.

Credit expansion, problem of currency expansion, 54; measures permitted by AAA, 55; affected by gold purchase, 57; relation to price raising, 58; RFC agency for, 60 ff.

Crime Prevention Compact Act, 136.

Crop Loan Act, 133.